NATO: THE TRANSATLANTIC BARGAIN

NATO:
THE TRANSATLANTIC
BARGAIN

by HARLAN CLEVELAND

HARPER & ROW, PUBLISHERS

NEW YORK, EVANSTON, AND LONDON

Contents

NORTH ATLANTIC
TREATY
ORGANIZATION

1 BELGIUM
2 CANADA
3 DENMARK
4 FRANCE
5 FED. REPUBLIC
  OF GERMANY
6 GREECE
7 ICELAND
8 ITALY
9 LUXEMBOURG
10 NETHERLANDS
11 NORWAY
12 PORTUGAL
13 TURKEY
14 UNITED KINGDOM
15 UNITED STATES

Preface

In the Paris suburb of Versailles, not long before NATO's headquarters moved to Brussels, a touring company put on Peter
Ustinov's aging allegorical play, *The Love of Four Colonels.* In
this short talky drama four officers—French, British, American
and Soviet colonels—vie for a lady's hand; the lady is perfection.
Each fails because perfection is unattainable, and Dr. Diabolikov,
who is Ustinov's version of the Devil, offers them a proposition.
They can, he says, go to sleep for a hundred years and awaken
with perfection in their grasp. As they debate the issue, the
Soviet officer says he is a pragmatist; he is interested not in
horizons but in breathing. The American is attracted to oblivion;
he is disgusted with his wife, and anyway he needs the rest. Yet
as he considers the choice, he thinks of an overriding reason to
stay awake. "Wherever you have a Russian," he says, "it's a good
idea to have an American."

In the Versailles production this line was greeted with spon-
taneous and sustained applause. A member of the cast said afterwards that it invariably evokes a cheer from French audiences,
even in cities where the Communist vote is strong.

There is a little mystery about this French version of *The Love
of Four Colonels.* In the original Ustinov version the American
elects slumber, and that sure-fire applause line nowhere appears.
But whatever its object and origin, the anonymous rewrite man
captured in a short declarative sentence what most Europeans,
and most Americans, know has been the practical basis for peace
in the generation since World War II. Persuading the Soviet
Union that military militancy would not pay has been, and
remains today, the broadest assignment of American diplomacy
and the biggest single charge on our federal budget. Five American Presidents, twelve United States Congresses, and a half a

hundred European governments have believed, and acted on the belief, that wherever you have a Russian, it's a good idea to have an American.

To people of "my" generation—I will lump them at age 50, which will please some of my contemporaries and outrage the rest—this policy was a radical departure from an isolationist past. In our half-century we have witnessed at first hand some raw history which we can neither deny nor escape—the extreme case of extremist nationalism, the trial and error of appeasement, the wearying tragedy of war, the exhilaration of recovery, and the healing effect of mutual commitments among like-minded nations of the Atlantic rim. A policy that combined deterrence with diplomacy, by combining fifteen nations in a peacetime Alliance, came to seem quite natural even though there had been nothing like it before.

But the lessons that led to formation of the North Atlantic Alliance are not easily learned from history books; history repeats itself so often because people cannot bring themselves to act on perceptions they have not learned for themselves. Such is the rate of change in this century that this Alliance was no sooner well established than it began to look old-fashioned, because it was well established.

Those Americans who set some store by Atlantic cooperation were challenged both by the young who doubted the need for cooperation against Russia and those with more years and higher incomes who doubted the need to spend all that money just on maintaining peace. In a time of danger we built a dam called NATO, but, they seemed to be wondering, since the lake above the dam is now so placid, do we really need that expensive old dam any more?

Beginning in the mid-1960s, in consequence, the cohesion of the Atlantic community was tested by half-a-dozen crises, some chronic and some acute. Some in each member nation gave up the Alliance for lost. But as things turned out, most of the relevant political forces in all the Atlantic nations rediscovered a vital interest in hanging together, for a rapidly changing set of purposes. How those purposes were changed, and what we learned in the process about the nature of international consultation, is the story told in this book.

This story of the self-renewal of an institution cannot be told with the structural imagery and elaborate blueprints we love to use about international affairs. Modern bureaucratic man is moved not by rhetoric but by reorganization; a political leader making a proposal for change has to propose a new bureau if he wants to be taken seriously. But the static images of desirable future structures are not very useful in describing what really happens in international relations, how allies work together by limited accretions to practical cooperation. My story is not about a grand design, but about a series of tough-minded bargains ✓ arrived at through a process called consultation.

*   *   *

The reason I elected myself to tell this story, and speculate on the policy for the 1970s which it suggests, is that I was there. "There" was the political headquarters of the Western Alliance in Paris and then in Brussels, representing the United States on the North Atlantic Council, from September 1965 to June 1969.

There is an ancient truism of government that where you stand depends on where you sit. To the historians of the American Presidency, nearly everything in the government seems to originate in and be decided by the White House, though anybody who has worked in Washington knows that quite a lot of interesting and important work goes on in other parts of the government. The story I have told about transatlantic politics has its own built-in myopias.

I have certainly overstressed the doings of the North Atlantic ⌐ Council and underemphasized the work of its many committees and of its military commanders and their planning staffs.

As a story about multilateral diplomacy, this book focuses on the places where the multilateral consultation occurs and tends to neglect the creative confusions of politics back in the capitals of the fifteen allies.

As a story about American government, the narrative is written from the perspective of a field operative, who participated in Washington's bureaucratic wars intermittently and from a distance—through two or three phone calls and half-a-dozen policy cables a day, and 22 trips to Washington in 45 months on the job. But if the ambassador a President sends to represent him abroad does not develop a somewhat different perspective from the President's Washington-based advisers, he might as well have stayed at home.

Since I worked in three administrations during the 1960s, it would require a whole chapter to list the colleagues in the United States government, and in other governments, from whom I learned whatever practical wisdom is found in this volume. The opportunity to watch three very different Presidents—John F. Kennedy, Lyndon B. Johnson, and Richard Nixon—fill the world's largest executive shoes was a lifetime of education in itself. The chance to work closely with perceptive and congenial public officials from the Cabinet and the White House to the "working" levels, creates such an embarrassment of obligations that I had best leave them collective and anonymous. In nearly four years in Europe, I never had a complaint about access to the Cabinet officers who were the source of my policy instructions. Despite Vietnam and other preoccupations, the relationship with two Secretaries of State, Dean Rusk and William Rogers, and three Secretaries of Defense, Robert McNamara, Clark Clifford, and Melvin Laird, was professionally stimulating and personally pleasant.

But the greatest unacknowledged debt is to the extraordinary group of men and women who staffed the United States Mission to NATO during my time there. For the fact that they were assembled together in Paris and Brussels at that moment in time, I will take some credit; for the quality of their work, and the skill and enthusiasm with which they worked together, the credit is collectively theirs. For special help in thinking through some of the intricate issues discussed in these pages, I am grateful to Philip J. Farley, William I. Cargo, Thomas W. Wilson, Timothy W. Stanley, Raymond Garthoff, Edward Streator, and Bruno B. A. Luzzatto. Betsy White and Vickie Vanderstadt in Brussels, Lelia Letherland in Syracuse, Nobu Masuda and Rita

Long in Honolulu all helped capture my words and make them into readable sentences. The Policy Institute of the Syracuse University Research Corporation, and Stephen K. Bailey, its Chairman, sheltered me during the period of gestation. The Council on Foreign Relations made the book financially possible and brought together under Paul Nitze's chairmanship a group of careful and creative critics.

*   *   *

To finish in Hawaii a book on East-West relations in Europe creates a semantic schizophrenia. The world is round, and each people's East is some other people's West. On the Atlantic side of America's personality, East is the Soviet Union and the communist states of Eastern Europe. In our Pacific incarnation, East is the Orient and Asia beyond. Somehow, whichever way we are facing, we Americans always style ourselves West. I have not tried in this book to invent less confusing synonyms for East and West in Europe; but I thought in fairness to my new friends at the University of Hawaii and its East-West Center I should make the confusion clear.

H.C.

Honolulu, Hawaii
November 1969

NATO: THE TRANSATLANTIC BARGAIN

Chapter I

The Marketplace of Destiny

Americans do not as a rule applaud what Andrei Gromyko, the Soviet Foreign Minister, says in the United Nations. But one sentence of his 1968 General Assembly speech is worth framing as a guide to U. S. foreign policy: "History takes revenge for forgetfulness," he declared, "if somebody deliberately forgets the significance of European affairs or neglects them . . ."

In a generation of effort, at a cost running up to one trillion dollars—that is, a thousand billion dollars—the United States and Canada and their European allies have kept the peace in Europe by preventing war. A nonevent, something that doesn't happen, is hard to define with clarity or greet with enthusiasm. But the consequence of *not* neglecting European affairs is a rather impressive slice of history: among the world's other regions only North America has been as free of shots fired in anger during the years since 1945.

What is the secret of this success? Certainly not an absence of danger, or of international rivalries, or of desperate men, or of pressure and provocation. The Second World War left Western Europe exhausted, disorganized, and vulnerable. Stalin, taking President Roosevelt at his word when he said at Yalta that he could not keep American troops in Europe for more than two years after the War, set about to absorb by force all the territory in Eastern and Central Europe which Russian troops occupied at the war's end, to subvert the governments of Western countries that inherited big Communist parties from the era of resistance to the Nazis, and at the same time to put pressure on Iran, Turkey, Greece and Berlin. The Western Communist parties, then faithful followers of the Kremlin's leadership, seemed a good bet to take or at least share power in several Western European nations—France, Italy, and perhaps others. No one knew whether the postwar Germans, defeated, deflated, and divided, would react in resignation or resentment.

Yet somehow the French and Italian communists were out-flanked. The British and the Americans stayed on the Continent. The "good Germans" prevailed in Western Germany. The Greek and Turkish governments did not fold under pressures from militant communists inside and just outside their borders. Europe recovered its economic strength, nourished by $14 billion of aid from the Marshall Plan and spurred by the early promise of supranational communities. Despite a quarter-century of pressures, threats, ultimatums, provocations and crises, there has been no war among, or armed attack on, the members of the North Atlantic Treaty Organization. Anyone with a smattering of modern European history can appreciate how extraordinary and unprecedented a piece of good news this is.

The picture as of 1970 is far from rosy, and most of this book will be about what is wrong and what might be done about it. But it would be unfair to the Europeans, and to ourselves, not to pause a moment to celebrate this enormous historic success. It helps tell us where we are, it establishes a baseline for next steps; the agony of this success is indeed the basic problem in this twenty-first year of the North Atlantic Alliance.

Something must have been done right. The early stress on a massive program of economic recovery, the psychological and economic lift of the Common Market, the curiously credible threat of strategic nuclear retaliation for tactical transgressions, the symbolic integration of NATO armies, the willingness of war-time allies to make an ally of West Germany without awaiting a final peace settlement, the long and ultimately successful search for an Atlantic "nuclear sharing" arrangement, the West's espousal of a sort of coexistence policy—each of these policies played its part. But shining through the military half-measures and the tepid ministerial communiqués was a moral solidarity that somehow made more out of what was objectively not enough. The real deterrent to Soviet ambitions (which with our present hindsight may never have been so fierce as they seemed) was this: by and large, with occasional and temporary exceptions which fortunately turned out not to be critical, the Atlantic allies stuck together.

*   *   *

The glue that has held the allies more or less together is a large, complex and dynamic bargain—partly an understanding among the Europeans, but mostly a deal between them and the United States of America. This book is about that bargain, and the process by which history's strongest and most effective alliance is, and will in the future have to be, kept politically acceptable by constant recalculation of the costs assumed and benefits received by each party to the deal.

The transatlantic bargain works because the bargaining goes on within a framework of common interest, perceived and acknowledged. The most sensitive techniques of consultation would not obscure fundamental conflicts of national interest; the sometimes egregious errors of diplomatic technique and timing cannot override the shared sense that the North Atlantic allies are in the same boat. Each year the mix of NATO defense forces and the character of allied political collaboration changes, adapting to the shifting technology of war and to change, real or apparent, in the tides of domestic politics in each of the fifteen NATO countries. But while the bargain changes, the constant is a consensus among allies that there has to be a bargain.

The North Atlantic Alliance is thus an organized controversy about who is going to do how much of what to carry into action the common perception, so obvious that it is seldom debated, that the Atlantic allies might hang separately if they don't hang together. The Treaty form of the deal is "We'll help defend you if you help defend us." But few Europeans take very seriously the notion that they need come to America's aid; and despite Secretary of State Dean Rusk's quite serious allusions to the Bering Straits as the "Western flank" of NATO, most Americans also think of NATO as essentially an arrangement to ensure the defense of Western Europe. The price of mutual help is self-help: "We Americans will help you Europeans, if you will (a) help defend yourselves, and (b) get on with building a united Europe."

Some Americans do not like to use words like "deal" and "bargain" in describing the Atlantic Alliance. International relations, they think, should be nobler than ward politics and more disinterested than the relations among rug merchants in a bazaar. The United States, they like to feel, keeps the peace in Europe as an act of enlightened self-interest—because we have twice learned that war in Europe sooner or later draws us in to our cost and our sorrow. To speak of bargains implies that if the Europeans don't defend themselves, our national interest in their defense is no longer engaged. But the raw political fact is that unless the Europeans show a lively interest in their own defense, it becomes politically impossible for a government in Washington to represent to its own people that we are partners in a collective security mission. And when we seem lonely, committed, and exposed, popular support drains away.

*   *   *

The arguments within the Atlantic Alliance center on fairness—how to share the burdens that are supposed to be borne together and the decisions that are supposed to be taken together. The two are of course closely related: in international as in domestic politics, there is a tendency over time for taxation and representation to come into balance. Those who are reluctant to take responsibility tend to be left out of the meetings where decisions are made; those who are thoroughly consulted beforehand are more likely to help carry out the agreed line of action— or, at a minimum, to make their approbation audible as the action develops.

Inside a working alliance, it always seems to be a time of testing. Churchill wrote that the history of any alliance was a history of mutual recrimination; Napoleon's success, to hear Napoleon tell it, came because he fought against the quarreling members of an alliance. Sometimes the difficulties with allies have made it hard for the participants in the internal battle to remember that NATO's adversary was supposed to be the Soviet Union and the Warsaw Pact. In NATO, "disarray" is sometimes another way of saying "Alliance at Work."

In each part of the transatlantic bargain—defense planning, nuclear strategy, trade and monetary policy, the management of East-West negotiations, the harmonization of "extra-NATO" policies, the common concern with the environment—the glue that holds the allies together is constantly being tested for viscosity and adhesive power. In the time I spent as U.S. Ambassador to NATO, from 1965 to 1969, the North Atlantic Alliance met and surmounted six major crises. Only one, the invasion of Czechoslovakia, was of external origin, though it set off another round of transatlantic bargaining inside the Alliance. Another, the series of Greek-Turkish crises, found its proximity fuze just outside the NATO defense system in Cyprus; but both the obligations to the Alliance and the NATO-committed forces of the two almost-belligerents were deeply engaged.

Otherwise the disorders of the late 1960s might best be described as trouble in the internal affairs of the West. General de Gaulle's attempt, starting in 1965, to extricate France from the NATO defense system without defecting from the Alliance as a political system and the U.S./U.K. proposals to withdraw NATO committed troops in 1967 (and also, though it hardly rates as a major crisis, Trudeau's decision in 1969 to eliminate most of the Canadian contribution) were internal ploys designed to change the club rules and adjust burdens by unilateral action. The "détente fever" of the late 1960s, to which the strong medicine of the Harmel Report had to be applied, was also essentially an internal disorder; the reasons for relaxation were still more to be found in Western wish-thinking than in Eastern behavior. Finally, the uncertainty about the Treaty's twentieth birthday generated a crisis which was again of internal origin.

If disagreements about issues outside the NATO defense system could dissolve the Alliance, then it would certainly have been dissolved during this period. Yet, despite Vietnam, despite colonial and aid problems in Africa and Asia, despite a three-year Six Day War in the Middle East, arguments among the allies about outside issues demonstrably do not split the Alliance. On such issues as these, there is no agreed presumption, only a wan and unilateral hope that the Western club will help a member who gets into trouble outside the West.

NATO's capacity to overcome these glue-dissolving crises is due to the simple fact that the "disarray" is each year on a different subject. The casual observer in the United States does not readily learn the reason for this—partly because Atlantic affairs are obscured by drama and violence in other continents not so well endowed with peacemaking machinery as Europe is, and partly because the mass media are alert for signs of sickness but allergic to evidence of health. Family fights are mostly worked out in the family. The disarray ("France Leaves NATO," "Turks Poised for Attack," "American Senator Announces U.S. Withdrawal," "Nordics Debate NATO Pullout," "Détente May Mean End of NATO") breaks through the surface of public consciousness from time to time. But the hard talk and real concessions that put things back together are complex, technical, and deliberately shielded from public view: no politician wants it widely remarked that he did not carry through on a well-publicized intention. Television reporters and newspaper editors are easily bored by evidence that controversy is being replaced by cooperation, and quickly turn their attention elsewhere—until the time comes for some new negotiation about how to share a critical decision or an allied burden. Then the "NATO in Disarray" headline is dusted off and the cycle begins again.

The antidote for the myopia of journalistic method is a glance at the perspective of history. In looking back at the period of my own day-to-day involvement in the North Atlantic Council, it is very obvious that in this citadel of the Establishment "there've been some changes made."

● Four years ago, France's withdrawal was widely thought to be the beginning of the end of NATO. Today, the fourteen other allies have demonstrated they can and will defend the treaty area—with or without France.

● Four years ago, NATO strategy was obsolete, its air defense outmoded, and its communications conventional. Today, the new strategy has been agreed among the Fourteen (leaving France out for the time being); a new (if already obsolescent) air defense system has been installed; and a NATO communications satellite is being manufactured for launching in early 1970.

● Four years ago, the transatlantic allies were still arguing about "nuclear sharing" and getting nowhere with the proposed Multilateral Force (the MLF). Today, in the Nuclear Planning Group, responsibility for nuclear plans and deployments is the subject of serious international consultation.

● During these years, despite all the talk about force reduction, the allies have continued to spend roughly the same percentage of their gross national product on their defense, and to commit roughly the same forces to NATO's emergency plans.

● Four years ago, there was a widespread illusion that Europe's comparative security meant the NATO defense system could be scrapped. Today, all fifteen allies have agreed that if there are to be negotiations with the Soviets and their friends, the Western allies had better be strong enough to negotiate, and should reduce their forces in Europe only as part of a pattern of mutual and balanced force reduction worked out with the members of the Warsaw Pact.

● Four years ago, both the French and the Soviets were preaching that the way to European peace and security was to break up "blocs," starting with our own. This is still talked about from time to time in desultory propaganda. But the NATO allies—all fifteen, including the French—have reconstituted NATO as an alliance that is also active in seeking practical peace arrangements for Europe.

● Four years ago, 1969 seemed a significant date to NATO's friends as well as its opponents: in that twentieth-birthday year any ally could give notice of withdrawal. But no ally did. NATO's agreed defense plans and projects already extend to the mid-1970s. And shocked by the invasion of Czechoslovakia, the fifteen Atlantic partners have pronounced their Alliance to be of "indefinite duration," and declared that "recent events" (meaning the invasion of Czechoslovakia) "have further demonstrated that its continued existence is more than ever necessary."

This record of the late 1960s cannot be extrapolated into the 1970s. The capacity of some Europeans to believe in East-West peace before it is negotiated, and the impatience of some Americans to pull back from overseas commitments, may show these four years to have been a temporary halt in the secular decline and fall of NATO. But as the 1970s begin, the opening balance shows the Alliance more durable, more effective, and more relevant than even its partisans would earlier have thought possible.

*　　　　*　　　　*

There is nothing automatic about the cooperation enjoined by the North Atlantic Treaty, established in the North Atlantic Treaty Organization, or inherent in a regional security system. The relationship is best seen as *a strong presumption of coopera-tion in the event of trouble*—or in the event of negotiations that affect all the members. Everything the North Atlantic allies do together, or fail to do together, enhances or erodes that presumption.

The presumption of cooperation is not merely words on paper; it takes the form of machinery for making some decisions together in peacetime and agreeing ahead of time to make more decisions together in a common emergency. Appointing a Supreme Commander (who, in peacetime, is a planner, not a commander) marks a tentative decision that nations will put their troops under his command in an emergency. But that is only a promise, a guess about the future behavior of sovereign governments, subject to their policy review at the time. Launching a NATO communications satellite for crisis consultation and for military command and control does not guarantee its common use in a common emergency. It builds the presumption that when the chips are down the club members will want to work together by talking to each other. Telling the North Atlantic Council that it should seek to improve the climate of East-West relations, so as to lead to negotiations with the Soviets about concrete issues like Berlin and Germany and frontiers and mutual reduction of forces, puts pressure on the politicians of each allied country to act in concert with politicians in other countries. But nothing *makes* them do so if their national interest in common action is not clear to them when the moment for common action comes. The consensus that has kept the allies from fighting each other, and has kept 7,000 U.S. nuclear weapons and about 300,000 U.S. troops in Europe, is fragile—the product of manner and method more than of law and treaty. Decisions like these have to be retaken many times, and are never taken forever. This political marketplace where bargains about a common destiny are made and broken is always open for unilateral or negotiated revision of mutual obligations. For these are sovereign nations, and the ultimate court of appeal is not their international relations but their domestic politics.

The reasons for acting together are plural. It is the nature of politics that men and groups of men can agree to act together on a "next step" without agreeing on why they are taking it; indeed, if the philosophy as well as the policy had to be agreed, cooperation among nations would be rare indeed.

Thus in this club we call the Atlantic Alliance, the European members tend to think of NATO as (*a*) the American commitment to their defense; (*b*) a framework within which it is politically acceptable for the Germans to be strong again; (*c*) a military system that makes their own defense efforts, otherwise ridiculously vulnerable to Russian superpower, an understandable part of a relevant whole; and (*d*) a chance—for small countries the main chance—to have some say in decisions affecting their own future, including decisions about the control of arms, the "German question," and the future of Europe.

In dealing with their friendly yet fractious and distant partner, the United States, all the other countries of the Alliance do have one thing in common: comparatively speaking, they are small and weak. The problem for smaller nations is to be taken seriously on big questions. For, to maintain themselves as primary objects of their citizens' loyalties, the politicians who govern each nation (and those who would like to govern next) must seem to have free and easy access to the places where "destiny decisions" are made, and to be participating actively in those decisions.

For the United States the problem is different. We know we are going to be involved in the big questions: the big question for us is who else is going to be willing to share some of the real responsibility. For us, therefore, the Alliance represents (*a*) an instrument for organizing joint action under "many flags"; (*b*) a device to help prevent armed conflict among our allies, which include most of the major participants in this century's two world wars, and other pairs (notably Greece and Turkey) which harbor deep mutual antagonisms; (c) the justification in our own politics for thorough involvement in the preventive phases of peace-and-security crises in Europe, which we learned in those two world wars to be essential to our national security; and (d) a forum in which to build consent for arrangements we make at the superpower level with the Russians, and for arrangements about the future of Europe, Germany, and Berlin, in which we think we had better be deeply involved.

Within this system of multiple motivations, continuous negotiation goes on—about how and whether to increase the presumption of emergency cooperation by elaborating the machinery of peacetime planning, and about who is going to do how much, how soon, about more-or-less common problems that arouse differential degrees of anxiety in the domestic politics of each ally.

For Europeans and Canadians, the essence of the transaction is that they bargain with their resources to buy a voice in "destiny decisions"—decisions on defense strategy and planning, on the sharing of nuclear tasks and risks, on the management of East-West relations, on arms control and disarmament, and (within rather narrow limits) on issues of peace and war outside the NATO defense perimeter. An American can turn the transaction around: the United States is trading bits and pieces of its sovereign discretion—on defense strategy and planning, on nuclear management, on arms control negotiations, on extra-Alliance issues—for various kinds of European and Canadian contributions to the common defense.

This is the transatlantic bargain, and the negotiating instrument is that bastard child of mutual suspicion and mutual trust called consultation.

Chapter II

The Golden Rule
of Consultation

The nature of allies is that they expect to be consulted. We cannot share responsibility without sharing sensitive information and without discussing policy decisions that affect our allies before the decisions are made. We also expect that once our allies understand and agree with a line of policy and action, they will raise the money, send the forces, or otherwise join in the action.

There is no magic answer to the ticklish relationship that results from these mutual expectations among the Atlantic allies. But the best antidote to uncoordinated stupidity among friends is long, candid, and often tedious talk about real problems. What keeps the principle of consultation alive, and the practice so lively, is the practical advantage it brings, especially to the country which starts the conversation on each topic. We Americans need it to keep our "destiny decisions" more or less in line with our friends' notion of what their destinies should be. And our allies need it to make sure they participate in the destiny they share with us; their entrance fee, like ours, is to discuss together before acting separately.

The only explicit reference to consultation in the North Atlantic Treaty is Article 4, which says "the Parties will consult together whenever, in the opinion of any of them, the territorial integrity, political independence or security of any of the Parties is threatened." Even so, a massive commitment to consultation is implicit in the very purpose and structure of the Treaty itself, as indicated in its other Articles. Signatories who have undertaken to settle their international disputes by peaceful means, "to refrain in their international relations from the threat or use of force," to strengthen their free institutions, to eliminate conflict in their international economic policies, to cooperate in "continuous and effectve self-help and mutual aid" in order to "maintain and develop their individual and collective capacity to resist armed attack," to consider an armed attack against one or more of them as an attack against them all and in these circumstances to take "forthwith, individually, and in concert with the other Parties, such action as [they deem] necessary, including the use of armed force, to restore and maintain the security of the North Atlantic area" have certainly engaged to discuss these matters continuously and intimately among themselves.

As the Alliance became the organization known as NATO, a doctrine of consultation began to emerge. It would be hard to improve even today on the generalizations agreed by the NATO Committee on the North Atlantic Community in 1951:

> The achievement of a closer degree of coordination of the foreign policies of the members of the North Atlantic Treaty, through the development of the "habit of consultation" on matters of common concern, would greatly strengthen the solidarity of the North Atlantic Community and increase the individual and collective capacity of its members to serve the peaceful purposes for which NATO was established. . . . In the political field, this means that while each North Atlantic government retains full freedom of action and decision with respect to its own policy, the aim should be to achieve, through exchanging information and views, as wide an area of agreement as possible in the formulation of policies as a whole.

> Special attention must be paid, as explicitly recognized in Article 4 of the Treaty, to matters of urgent and immediate importance to the members of NATO, and to "emergency" situations where it may be necessary to consult closely on national lines of conduct affecting the interests of members of NATO as a whole. There is a continuing need, however, for effective consultation at an early stage on current problems, in order that national policies may be developed and action taken on the basis of a full awareness of the attitudes and interests of all the members of NATO. While all members of NATO have a responsibility to consult with their partners on appropriate matters,

a large share of responsibility for such consultation necessarily rests on the more powerful members of the Community.

Five years later, NATO's second set of "Three Wise Men" reinforced the "pressing requirement for all members to make consultation in NATO an integral part of the making of national policy." But five years of trying had clarified not only the need for consultation but also its inherent dilemma. On the one hand, said the Wise Men, "collective discussion is . . . a means to the end of harmonizing policies. Where common interests of the Atlantic Community are at stake, consultation should always seek to arrive at timely agreement on common lines of policy and action." On the other hand, "There are, of course, certain practical limitations to consultation . . ." including "the hard fact that ultimate responsibility for decision and action still rests on national governments. It is conceivable that a situation of extreme emergency may arise when action must be taken by one government before consultation is possible with the others."

The Wise Men did the best they could to resolve this practical dilemma in negotiated words:

the essential thing is that on all occasions and in all circumstances, member governments, before acting or even before pronouncing, should keep the interests and the requirements of the Alliance in mind. . . . A member government should not without adequate advance consultation, adopt firm policies or make major political pronouncements on matters which significantly affect the Alliance or any of its members, unless circumstances make such prior consultation obviously and demonstrably impossible.

This exhortation applied not only to the NATO defense area as such, but to the wider world. "NATO should not forget that the influence and interests of its members are not confined to the area covered by the Treaty, and that common interests of the Atlantic Community can be seriously affected by developments outside the treaty area."

Another five years passed, and the allied governments struggled with the same practical dilemma in its nuclear incarnation. At the NATO Ministerial meeting held in Athens during May 1962, the members agreed on "guidelines" about recourse to nuclear weapons in self-defense. They called for consultation about the use of nuclear weapons, but necessarily left a loophole—time and circumstances permitting—almost as wide as the commitment. The United States and the United Kingdom sweetened the pill by agreeing to consult with their NATO allies—again if time permits—about the use of nuclear weapons anywhere in the world.

And five years after that, in December 1967, the allies again tried to put into words how they would reconcile their mutual trust with their mutual suspicion. In its *Report on the Future Tasks of the Alliance,* the North Atlantic Council first stapled defense and détente together, and then tried to say how the Alliance might deal with the growing evidence that each NATO member was pressing for détente in its own way and with its own special partners in Eastern Europe. This time, to keep the French on board, the negative side of the consultation dilemma was stated first, but the same two-faced deity was worshipped and glorified:

> As sovereign states the Allies are not obligated to subordinate their policies to collective decision. The Alliance affords an effective forum and clearing house for the exchange of information and views; thus, each of the Allies can decide his policy in the light of close knowledge of each other's problems and objectives. To this end the practice of frank and timely consultations needs to be deepened and improved. Each Ally should play its full part in promoting an improvement in relations with the Soviet Union and the countries of Eastern Europe, bearing in mind that the pursuit of détente must not be allowed to split the Alliance. The chances of success will clearly be greatest if the Allies remain on parallel courses, especially in matters of close concern to them all; their actions will thus be all the more effective.

The principle, then, is deceptively simple: friends and allies should consult each other—at a minimum to avoid unpleasant surprises among them, at a maximum to align their national policies or make collective decisions. That is what fifteen countries have agreed to, by legislation, practice, and precedent in twenty years of operating under the North Atlantic Treaty.

Yet each international consultation on any real issue faces

enormous difficulties. Each ally wants to be consulted about decisions by others affecting its interests. But each ally wants to reserve its right on particular matters to be secretive, to avoid consulting at all, or to resolve its own uncertainties before listening to certainties of others less responsible for action. It is the nature of responsible governments to want to consult about problems vital to others, while "keeping options open" on matters vital to themselves. Like Janus of the Romans, the modern god of international consultation faces in both directions: while observing the acts or omissions of others, he also watches you.

If the essence of the matter, for each party, is trading its own discretion for its allies' performance, it might be expected that the two sides to the bargain would apply different standards to the consultation process. They do.

Our declaratory policy is the Golden Rule of Consultation. The Platonic form of this rule was authoritatively expressed by Vice President Humphrey to the North Atlantic Council on April 7, 1967:

> To put it bluntly, how do you make sure that our negotiations with the Soviets—as on disarmament, on non-proliferation, or anti-ballistic missiles—do not do violence to your vital interests?
>
> And conversely, how do we make sure that the initiatives and negotiations of our allies do not adversely affect our own vital interests and responsibilities?
>
> We have a way of safeguarding and harmonizing our interests as traffic quickens through the "Open Door."
>
> It is by consultation through this Council. . . .
>
> Our presence in the midst of the Alliance bears witness to our firm commitment to act as faithful partners to our allies.
>
> And if we follow the Golden Rule—that each of us consult as soon, as often, and as frankly as he would wish the others to consult—the Alliance will prove to be the midwife of more hopeful times.

The American consulters, however, have had to get used to a double standard. Just as, in the United Nations, the membership holds the United States to higher standards of political and military behavior than it applies to smaller or less developed nations or even to the Soviet Union, so in NATO our allies tend to assume that we have more of an obligation to start the conversation than they do. We try to hold them to the Golden Rule of Consultation; but in practice the U.S. government recognizes with realism and tolerance that it really is up to the big members of the club to set the tone and timing of consultation on big issues.

We consult more because we do more. (Whether we consult more proportionately to what we could consult about is more doubtful.) Our purpose in consulting is usually to build consent for a line of policy—and we happen to have more lines of policy, on more subjects, to build consent around. We are more active in other continents—except possibly in Africa. We necessarily take more leadership in other international forums, such as the United Nations, and the Geneva disarmament talks. We are the largest single contributor to half a hundred international organizations. Most countries can afford not to worry about how most international decisions come out—except when they threaten worldwide catastrophe. There are very few international subjects on which the United States can afford that luxury—and even on those, the nations which are directly involved often hope to involve us. Indeed, our attempts to maintain an even-handed neutrality on all sorts of two-sided rivalries around the world subject the United States to sometimes bitter criticism from both sides.

Because of these wide responsibilities, moreover, we maintain an intelligence-gathering network that operates world-wide, and in outer space as well. Our allies expect us to be a primary source of information about whatever is "hot" anywhere in the world, including Europe and the Mediterranean; a degree of access to U.S. information is indeed part of what they get for their commitments to NATO.

Even within the NATO defense system, our actions and inactions tend to set the tone for the other participants, simply because we are the largest contributor of the best forces. It was enormously in our interest to bring about allied agreement on the "new strategy," including the concepts of "political warning," flexible response, and managed escalation; prior to such agreement, our European allies could tell themselves our strategic nuclear deterrent was the answer to their security problem, and avoid the hard choices required to build adequate conventional forces themselves. If we had awaited European initiative to start that consultation, we would be waiting still.

*   *   *

In the current practice of the North Atlantic Council and its subordinate bodies, "consultation" is a flexible word. It can mean imparting information unilaterally; exchanging information bilaterally or multilaterally; notifying others of national decisions already taken, but without expecting any reaction on their part; notifying others of decisions already taken, in such a way as to build consent for them; consulting in advance on national actions that affect the interests of others; consulting internationally to ascertain in advance the possible reaction to a national decision not yet made (that is, as an input to the national decision itself); consulting in advance on a matter lending itself to separate parallel national actions by others; or consulting for the purpose of arriving at a decision which by its nature must be taken or carried into action collectively.

Most of the arguments about allied consultation result from decisions by individual allies to misplace a topic along this spectrum. "Are you telling us or consulting us?" is the question most frequently asked when a topic is presented for discussion in the North Atlantic Council. The real answer often requires the questioner to ask himself another question in turn: "Do I want to take the responsibility of being consulted for real—and contracting some obligation to act on (or to be restricted by) my own advice?"

The tabulation on pages 22-23 shows how some representative subjects that have arisen in the North Atlantic Council are spread across the spectrum of consultation. At one end we find the collective decisions required to maintain and modernize NATO's defense program that require real accommodation among national points of view—for example, defense strategy and civilian political guidance to the NATO military; the joint spending of common funds (for military constructions and command-and-control communications); and actions, such as the selection of a Supreme Commander, that must be seen as taken collectively even if the effective decision has already been made by the United States.

At the other end of the spectrum are reports made as a matter of courtesy on responsibilities unilaterally assumed by individual allies in the non-NATO world; Vietnam is the most durable case in point.

In between, it is a question of the judgment, taste, and style of each government how each subject will be handled in the NATO consultation process—whether the nation starting the consultation will be "notifying" or "consulting"—or a mixture of both. When subjects touching the vital interests of all allies become operational, allies must in their own interest "consult for real"; before that, governments can afford to be more casual about telling each other what they are thinking. Thus, except for one spasm in the late 1950s, discussions in the North Atlantic Council about the future of Europe, and about arms control arrangements in Europe, were rather desultory until a couple of years ago. Then the growing enthusiasm for détente and the assumption that practical negotiations with the Soviets on European issues might be just around the corner began to require serious and prolonged consultations, and real efforts to reach near-unanimous allied policies on the coordination of East-West contacts and the development of proposals for mutual force reduction in Europe.

*   *   *

A few weeks after the invasion of Czechoslovakia, the United States government decided to send into the Black Sea on a "routine" trip two armed destroyers from the U.S. Sixth Fleet in the Mediterranean. The visit was in some sense routine. We had made a practice of sending warships through the Dardanelles every six months or so, simply to make the point that the Black Sea is water just as international as the Pacific Ocean—or the Gulf of Tonkin. But given the Soviet occupation of Czechoslovakia, the apparent threat of similar treatment for Rumania, a Black Sea power, and the stern NATO warning that any further Soviet moves "would create an international crisis with grave consequences," the political environment for this "routine" visit was far from ordinary.

When plans for the destroyers' visit were checked by the Navy with the State Department, it fell to me to suggest that we consult our allies about it ahead of time. The suggestion, made first by telephone and then by telegram from Brussels, was not well received: the clinching argument in the Washington decision seemed to be the circular reasoning that if we consulted in NATO about the visit, it would be harder later on (when predictably the Soviets would complain we were being provocative) to allege that we regarded the visit as previously scheduled, normal, and nothing to get excited about. The scene then played itself out: the warships steamed in, the Soviets loudly complained, some of our allies asked why we had not consulted them, and I referred them to the State Department and the U.S. Navy. It was a rather minor flap, but one of our Mission's argumentative messages made a point which could be generalized: What would we have thought if the United Kingdom or Italy had sent two destroyers into the Black Sea that week without talking to us first?

*   *   *

Even close allies do not consult each other any more than they have to. For each government, there are clear and present inhibitions to sharing with others its analysis of a delicate situation, its information about diplomatic contacts, and especially the opportunity to influence its own national policy.

The reluctance to consult for reasons of security is often thoroughly justified. Premature leakage of a government's point of view on a sensitive matter may deeply affect national policy, or the government's ability to carry through what it thinks should be its policy. Conversation with some allies may leak to other allies; what is told to allies may be passed along to non-allies or even, through espionage, to potential enemies; leaks from a private consultation often reverberate in the domestic politics of the nation which started the consultation. Moreover, each government has some intelligence sources which may dry up or be compromised if generally revealed.

THE SPECTRUM OF NATO CONSULTATION

Exchange of information:

Notification (after the fact)

Report on NATO Ministers' visits to Eastern European capitals
Intelligence reports on what has already happened

Analysis

U.S. briefings on Vietnam
U.K. briefings on East-of-Suez pullback
Sharing, in North Atlantic Council, national prognoses on threats to the
    peace (Middle East, Berlin, etc.)
Discussion among disarmament experts
Discussion among regional experts

Consultation about national actions:

Notification as a matter of general
interest (just to keep the record
clear)

Fleet visits
U.K. decision to negotiate a Friendship Treaty with the Soviets
U.S. base negotiations affecting U.S. forces in the European area
Annual consultation on U.N. General Assembly agenda items

Consent-building notification (after
the fact)

Advance word on U.S. reaction to Soviet missiles in Cuba
Explanation of U.S. intervention in Dominican Republic
Explanation of U.S. ABM decision (done in Nuclear Planning Group)
West German decision to hold Presidential election in Berlin

Advance consultation on national
actions

U.S.-Soviet strategic arms limitation talks
Belgian disarmament talks with Poland
Discussions on visits of national leaders to U.S.S.R.

Consultation ("before and during" with a view to parallel national actions and attitudes:

Stoppage of contacts with the Warsaw Five, after the invasion of Czechoslovakia

Later resumption of such contacts

Disarmament issues arising in Geneva (ENDC) talks—e.g., Seabeds

Non-Proliferation Treaty

Middle East crisis consultation

Relations with Malta

Periodic Berlin crises

Consultation ("before and during" with a view to collective action:

Reaction of "the Fourteen" to French withdrawal from NATO

Force planning, strategic concepts

Appointment of NATO Commanders

Guidelines for the use of tactical nuclear weapons

Report on the Future Tasks of the Alliance (1967)

Declaration on Mutual Force Reductions (June 1968)

Ministerial Communiqués on post-Czechoslovakia NATO actions (November 1968 and January 1969)

Technical improvements in collective defense (air defense system, NATO Communications Satellite)

Budgetary and burden-sharing decisions:

Infrastructure (common-funded military construction)

Civil and Military Budgets (common-funded operating expenses)

The principal constraint on Alliance consultation is the desire of each government to "keep its options open." What is really kept open thereby is the option to act unilaterally, without having to take possible allied objections into account—until afterwards. But it is difficult to keep the option of unilateralism open without closing the option of acting in concert with partners. Until recently we managed naval cooperation in the Mediterranean without affecting the ability of the individual navies to go into action unilaterally in situations short of general war. But in the process, NATO governments with forces in the Mediterranean were deprived of the option of operating multilaterally in peacetime, each using a part of its forces together with NATO-committed units of others. Yet this might be just what the President would want to do in the most likely situations—those short of general war.

The ambition to keep options open tends to vary with size and national strength. The larger NATO members tend to resist specifying how the allies would act together in war, or how the Alliance should make a peace settlement in Europe. The smaller members feel they have no realistic option of independent action, and they concentrate on trying to commit their larger partners (especially, of course, the United States) to intimate consultation in future emergencies.

A further inhibition to consultation is to be found in the dynamics of bureaucratic decision-making, particularly in the biggest national bureaucracies. The repetitive pattern in a national capital is something like this: after several months of hard bargaining among the Foreign Office, the Ministry of Defense, the military Chiefs of Staff, perhaps other specialized agencies, and the relevant parliamentary or congressional leaders, a fragile compromise is arrived at and adopted as national policy. The suggestion (often from the Ambassador to NATO) that a delicate bureaucratic balance achieved with great difficulty should be subjected to the views of fourteen other governments in the North Atlantic Council naturally seems a form of madness to the committed participants in the decision. Sometimes, however, the losers in an internal argument see a chance to argue some more if allies are consulted, and become sudden converts to NATO consultation.

A final inhibition worth mentioning is the one best grounded in the real world of multilateral diplomacy: most NATO members are generally unwilling to act outside their own immediate region. The nation originating a "consultation" does not want to waste time talking to allies who will remain inactive even if they agree. To their desire to be consulted must always be opposed the uncomfortable corollary question: If we can agree together on a common attitude, who is prepared to do something about it? The desire of some allied governments for the bombing halt in North Vietnam was met by Secretary of State Dean Rusk with the conversation-stopping question: If we do stop the bombing, what will you then do to get Hanoi to negotiate? In a contrasting case, consultations leading up to the post-Czechoslovakia meeting of NATO Ministers in November 1968 were designed to ascertain which governments were seriously prepared to do something about building up their contributions to the NATO defense system and how much. The result was more than a billion dollars of new effort, which no government was prepared to undertake on its own initiative, but which all could undertake together in response to the "collective initiative" of NATO.

*　　　*　　　*

The principle and practice of NATO consultation survives these almost fatal inhibitions because the advantages to be derived from the practice of partnership with allies so often countervail.

One advantage is that consulting gets other allies engaged— even if there is never a full agreement on an assessment of a situation or a policy to be followed. The fact, or even the appearance, of consultation keeps open the option to act multilaterally if the situation later requires this. It helps choke off complaints in which governments hide their substantive objections behind criticism of the procedure for eliciting them. Such complaints can seriously complicate the carrying out of national policies. Complaints by European governments about U.S. unilateralism reverberate in American domestic politics, and provide a weapon for anti-American elements in the domestic politics of European countries.

In the NATO defense system, moreover, intimate consultation is increasingly a technological imperative. Faster aircraft, tactical nuclear missiles, satellite communications, progress in weather forecasting, the rising costs of increasingly sophisticated equipment—these and a hundred other consequences of scientific and technological change require more rapid, more explicit, and more highly-organized arrangements for coordinating allied defense efforts even in peacetime. Moreover, the speed with which a modern crisis can escalate to serious proportions is so great that whole new systems of crisis management are required if we are to be able to act in partnership with our allies in a crisis.

On the political side, the period of "détente politics" preceding the Soviet invasion of Czechoslovakia illustrated the dangers and complexities when every ally is reaching for a separate kind of peace with the Russians in Europe. As we returned in 1969, after the invasion, to the search for a better climate of East-West relations, more intimate and earlier consultation became the simple alternative to fatal rifts in the North Atlantic Alliance itself.

Beyond the advantages to our foreign policy of consulting early and often, there are ways in which international consultations are helpful at home, in Washington and in the country. In a fundamental sense, the U.S. government consults its allies because it increasingly needs partners in order to have a foreign policy at all. Commitments considered to be unilateral are less and less defensible in American public opinion. Any element of American foreign policy has a better chance of solid bipartisan support in the United States if able and willing partners are seen to be at our side. To the extent we want credible partners—that is, partners who do more than listen politely to the case for U.S. unilateral action—we have to create a sense of participation by "levelling" with them.

We do want credible partners, more than ever. The Vietnam war has produced a much greater desire in American politics for what one writer calls "a sense of joint enterprise with other nations rather than a sense of the American flag in solitude and, often as not, in trouble." It is hard to know just when we crossed the line separating the bulk of our history, when operating under the American flag abroad was the most popular thing to do, from the modern era when peacekeeping under the U.N. flag (in Korea, Cyprus, and the Congo) or the NATO flag (in Europe, the Atlantic Ocean, and the Mediterranean Sea), or the OAS flag (around Cuba and in the Dominican Republic) seems to be the best way to avoid domestic trouble about overseas commitments. But we have crossed that great divide for sure and certain. In consequence, it has become as important at home as it is abroad for us to consult, and to be seen to be consulting, with others who might join in bearing troublesome burdens in future emergencies.

The very existence of a NATO consultation is sometimes a factor in domestic decisions. Prior to the Soviet action in Czecho-slovakia, a persuasive argument used by pro-NATO senators against the idea that we should unilaterally withdraw U.S. troops from Europe was the fact that we were at that moment engaged with our allies in a multilateral effort to draw the Warsaw Pact nations into negotiations about balanced and mutual force reduction in Europe. The international consultation on that subject was in fact begun partly so that it could be used that way in domestic arguments.

This suggests the heretical notion that consulting with for-eigners improves the quality of our own decisions. By consulting, often informally, before the bureaucratic bargains have been struck and our own policy has been frozen, the U.S. government secures a valuable input into its own decision-making process; simply imagining what various kinds of foreigners are likely to say is but a pale substitute for the real thing. By actually consult-ing, we help ourselves to make decisions that avoid at least the obvious complaints or opposition from our friends.

By consulting with others before reaching a decision, a govern-ment also forces itself to think harder about what it is doing and why it is doing it. Once NATO at U.S. initiative had created in the Nuclear Planning Group a forum which required that the use of tactical nuclear weapons be professionally discussed among responsible and increasingly knowledgeable Defense Ministers of allied governments, we had to think much harder ourselves about the rationale for the presence and potential use of tactical nuclear weapons in Europe. The result has been some brilliant analytical work, better than anything produced in Washington on this subject prior to the self-created requirement for international consultation.

It is tempting to speculate whether decisions on other matters which were not subjected to serious international consultation—the successive escalations in Vietnam are again the obvious example—would have been better decisions if we had had to discuss them with foreigners. Even with a complex and many-sided decision-making process, it is comparatively easy for any government to kid itself; it is always much harder to kid foreigners.

*   *   *

The advantages of consultation are bound to be more obvious to the full-time consulters, such as an Ambassador at NATO head-quarters, than to officials preoccupied with executive decision-making and congressional salesmanship in Washington. Indeed, the best reason for conducting consultations multilaterally in the North Atlantic Council and its subordinate bodies is that the full-time practitioners of multilateral diplomacy develop a "habit of consultation"—that is, they get in the habit of moving slightly beyond their formal instructions.

In a typical case the discussion starts with known governmental positions that are clearly inconsistent with each other and will, if maintained, create a stalemate. But the study of these positions, when they are all laid on the same conference (or luncheon) table, enables each representative to make a judgment about how much his own instructions would have to be bent in order to meet his colleagues'—if they succeed in bending their instructions too. Each representative then reports to his government that a new proposition, not contained in anybody's instructions, might just make it possible to secure agreement. Each representative, in the elementary exercise of bureaucratic caution, attributes this composite formula to one or more *other* governments, and most of our allies are likely to attribute it to the United States. With-

out representatives who are willing to operate in that diplomatic
no-man's-land beyond their formal instructions, the efficiency of
collective diplomacy would be greatly reduced, and governments
might just as well send messages directly from capital to capital
even on issues that involve many nations.

In conference diplomacy the chairman and the international
secretariat play a crucial role. In NATO, unlike the United Nations
organizations, the Secretary General and his subordinates normally chair the meetings of government representatives; the
Secretary General is chairman of the Council even when the Foreign Ministers personally sit as the national members. Successful
mediation by a sensitive and perceptive chairman (the Secretary
General during my time at NATO, Manlio Brosio of Italy, was
certainly that) helps the representatives put together on a personal basis a consensus which they will then try to sell, each to
his own government. The international staff is also in a position
to provide working documents which (even when they are in fact
derived from consultations with one or a few delegations) have a
sufficient aura of neutrality to serve as an uncontroversial framework for multilateral talk and Alliance action.

The unusual degree of political intimacy maintained among
the Permanent Representatives on the NATO Council, and among
their key functional subordinates, is partly the product of pro-
pinquity. In most international organizations the representative
of a government will not be housed with the other representatives,
or with the international staff. In NATO's Brussels headquarters,
the secretariat, all national delegations, and representatives to
the Military Committee as well, are housed in a single building.
For the U.S. Ambassador to NATO, responsible representatives
of fourteen governments are never more than a five-minute walk
away; it takes a minute and a half to reach the Secretary General's
office.

Each nation which starts a consultation on any subject faces
recurring questions of consultation technique: multilateral versus
bilateral, formal versus informal, all versus some allies, early
versus late.

One of the chief reasons for consulting multilaterally through
a body like the North Atlantic Council is simple efficiency. It is

arithmetically much easier for a government to impart information or solicit action from fourteen other countries around the table in multilateral conference, than to do exactly the same thing bilaterally through fourteen embassies in one capital or (with inevitable differences in style and even content) in somewhat differing ways in fourteen capitals. (Mathematically, a network of 105 separate relationships is involved to achieve consensus among fifteen allies when using only bilateral consultation.) Without the multilateral conference, as some forgotten phrase-maker put it, diplomacy would be like mathematics without the zero.

The distinction between bilateral and multilateral techniques of diplomatic discourse can easily be overdrawn. Even a regular ambassador in a traditional embassy finds nowadays that a large proportion of his dealings on policy matters with the government to which he is accredited consists of issues for which the real venue is a multilateral body—a U.N. session, an alliance meeting, or a technical conference on satellite communications or meteorology or tariffs or teaching or tunafish. The United States government is represented at more than 600 such conclaves every year. The fact is that the major questions in modern international relations increasingly come to a head on multilateral occasions, but much of the persuasion and compromising has to be done bilaterally, either in home capitals or behind the scenes between delegations at the international meeting. In practice, therefore, the two techniques are best regarded not as alternatives, but as mutually reinforcing.

The U.S. Foreign Service has learned much in recent years about playing back and forth between capitals and NATO headquarters on Alliance issues. Nearly every substantive telegram from the U.S. Mission to NATO is repeated to embassies in some allied capitals; perhaps a dozen a day are repeated to all allied capitals. Thus when one or more posts are asked for a special effort on any particular NATO topic, the background is already there in the memory of officers and the files of the embassy.

The larger governments in the Alliance like to show their people that they are doing business directly with the United

States—at least when they are getting their way. When their proposals are unlikely to prevail, even the major allies want the outcome to look as NATO-inspired as possible. The smaller members favor multilateral consultation nearly all the time. They do not have "hot lines" to Washington, as the British and Germans (and of course the Soviets) do, and if they did they would still have no confidence that anybody on the Washington end of the line would have the time or patience in an emergency to listen to a small country's opinion uncoordinated with the views of its neighbors. Moreover, they sometimes feel diffident in bilateral discussions of really major issues, tongue-tied by the disparity in size and power between the United States and themselves. In dealing with the American Leviathan, there is both safety and influence in numbers.

Even when an issue arises essentially with one or two allies, we often find advantage in conducting bilateral talks within a framework of multilateral consideration in the NATO Council. A case in point, as we shall later see, was the long NATO consultation about the Non-Proliferation Treaty.

The degree of formality required for effective consultation also varies greatly with the topic and the stage of negotiation. The more the consultation is intended to "show," the more formal it has to be. Sensitive subjects and subjects not yet ripe for full-dress consideration are best handled informally.

A wide variety of techniques has been developed in NATO for "informalizing" the discussion of a topic too sensitive, or too unripe, for formal consideration in the North Atlantic Council itself. They range from "informal meetings" of the Council (made without a record, and sometimes held in the Secretary General's private conference room), through subordinate bodies such as the Political Advisers, the Economic Advisers, and the Defense Review Committee (which can similarly operate "informally" and make even smaller waves), to lunches and teas and after-dinner discussions, for which many opportunities present themselves in the social life of a diplomatic community. The presence of a Tournedos Rossini, a platter of French cheeses, or a post-prandial liqueur seems to make possible the kind of frankness and real negotiation that is seldom seen in a regular international committee meeting even when it is secret—and would never be seen in a public session.

The Council's Permanent Representatives in Brussels have developed the habit of a weekly lunch. Here, by tradition, the diplomatic wraps are off. Everyone is talking in his personal capacity, obviously reflecting his government's thinking but also criticizing it on occasion. Conversation is usually limited to one or two major subjects, and is guided by whomever happens to be host for the lunch. Some of the frankest and most useful multilateral discussions to which the United States is a party occur on these occasions.

Not every subject needs to be discussed with every ally. The "PermRep lunches" normally include less than a complete roster of NATO members—the tradition is that only ambassadors are invited and nobody substitutes if the ambassador is out of town. Even within the formal structure of NATO, less-than-fifteen bodies have been an increasingly evident feature of the political landscape. The Nuclear Planning Group has seven or eight Defense Ministers; the "open-ended" Malta Group normally draws only seven or eight nations; and the whole NATO defense program is of course supervised by the fourteen-nation Defense Planning Committee—a euphemism for the North Atlantic Council meeting without France to transact defense business. Beyond these officially blessed arrangements, it is always possible to gather around a table whichever delegations are really essential to a discussion, at the initiative of one of them or of the Secretary General. A contemporary example is the "Eurodinners" at which the European Defense Ministers meet, sometimes to prepare to bargain collectively with their transatlantic partners in NATO.

*   *   *

Whether to consult early or late is, again, not subject to rule-making; the answer depends so much on what the topic is. In general, if the consultation is "real"—in the sense that the nation starting the conversation is prepared to modify its views on the basis of the discussion it starts—the matter should be opened as early as possible. Where true consultation is not intended, but consent needs to be built for a decision taken, the best practice is to tell allies about the decision before they read it in the newspapers, but not so long before as to create an opportunity to object.

The fact that a consultation starts early does not necessarily make it "real." Bogus consultation can be started early too, and consultees later informed that other counsels (even the advice of other allies) prevailed. This kind of thing is still usually better than no consultation at all. But it is a trifle cold-blooded for a government like ours, which resists a reputation for Machiavellian behavior.

The United States has a special problem on any issue involving negotiation with the Soviet Union. If we discuss with the allies a question that depends on U.S.-Soviet agreement, before it is clear the Soviets want to discuss it seriously, we cannot later depend on the reactions we get from our allies because they will not have been treating the problem as a serious one.

There need be no harm in discussing a problem before it is ripe, and there is usually some harm in a record of not discussing it until just before it ripens. Most international arguments about consultation stem from a sense of surprise, not from policy objections. Surprise can normally be avoided by continuous information and consultation. But no government can assume that in early discussions of a vital issue it is ascertaining the dependable and responsible reactions of allied governments. Governments, like people, do not often address policy questions in a serious way until they are unavoidable.

Chapter III

The Doctrine of Deterrence

Most of the day-to-day consultation in the North Atlantic Alliance, these past twenty years, has been about how to share the burden of building and keeping up to date the national military forces that are committed to NATO if the common emergency envisaged by the Treaty comes to pass. This is the substance of the Western defense bargain with its crises and compromises, its arguments about troops and technology, budgets and balance of payments. Yet this part of the Atlantic transaction rests on a more basic and even more controversial bargain about how decisions are going to be shared. In the environment of nuclear uncertainty, the decisions our allies most want to share are those that commit nations to war and expose their peoples to destruction.

A threat to the NATO defense area—Western Europe, the Mediterranean, continental United States and Canada, and the ocean between—is by common consent a nuclear emergency. In the other parts of the world, some thirty armed conflicts since the "last war" have demonstrated how much room there is for conventional arms in this so-called nuclear age. Kashmir, the recurring Arab-Israel war, and border conflicts in three continents are evidence enough that the technology of Armageddon does not inhibit small-scale wars with modern but non-nuclear explosives. (The strategic confrontation of the great powers may indeed operate to encourage regional conflict in peripheral areas by limiting the direct intervention of the nuclear powers.) Even when one or more of the nuclear powers is involved, the constraints on nuclear weaponry are obviously very strong. From 1950 to 1953 the United Nations forces took a quarter of a million casualties in Korea, and the United States alone has taken an even greater number in Vietnam. In neither case were nuclear weapons considered a serious option; when a Presidential candidate mentioned using nuclear bombs against North Vietnam the remark was widely taken to disqualify him for the office he sought. Only when the United States and the U.S.S.R. confronted each other directly—as they did once, in the Cuba missile crisis—have strategic nuclear weapons become relevant to conflict outside of Europe.

It is different in Europe, and the difference is NATO. Through binding treaty commitment the United States is for defense purposes a European power; thus a European confrontation is always potentially a nuclear confrontation. Such an environment is without precedent—no defense partnership in history has had to reckon with escalation to oblivion. This is why arguments about NATO strategic doctrine are so central to the whole Atlantic relationship. It is why the issue of a European nuclear force was so sensitive, the controversy about "nuclear sharing" so bitter, the dispute about the Multilateral Force (MLF) so passionate, and the success of the Nuclear Planning Group such good news. But as backdrop to that story, we need first a layman's theory of nuclear deterrence.

*   *   *

In recent years Americans have been so drenched with publicity about war and peace with Hanoi that we have been in some danger of mistaking the Vietnam war for the main security issue facing the government and people of the United States. It is not. The Soviet Union is still the only nation which has the physical capacity to destroy the United States—even if we tried to destroy the Soviets first. Likewise, the Soviet leaders have to keep in mind, twenty-four hours a day, the ultimate fact of their national life: the United States has the physical capacity to destroy the Soviet Union, even if they try to destroy us first. Underneath all the talk about pre-emption, retaliation, ballistic missile defenses, multiple independently targeted re-entry vehicles, over-the-horizon radar, and lightning-fast computerized analytical systems to give the President a few minutes instead of a few moments in which to make an apocalyptic decision, one unyielding fact remains: nobody in either nation has worked out a way to catch enough of the other's incoming ballistic missiles to change the simultaneous equation of annihilation.

Our ultimate sanction, we have long told ourselves, is the threat to destroy the Soviet Union in punishment for the high crime of aggression. The early-1950s doctrine of massive retaliation was about as simple as that. But once both sides have an ultimate sanction, the calculus is radically different: if willing the destruction of the Soviet Union entails willing also the destruction of Western Europe and the United States, that antiseptic phrase "strategic exchange" really means mutual suicide— clearly a very last resort, not by itself a foolproof deterrent to limited aggression.

The consequence is a *pax ballistica*—an old-fashioned balance of power with the newest-fangled weapons of all. No balance that is technologically so dynamic could be described as stable. Yet the strategic nuclear stand-off does set a limit to the ultimate pursuit of national policy by military means, and that is a historical "first."

Until our time, war has been limited only by men's capacity to wage and sustain it. The absolute destruction of the enemy's capacity to resist has long been the image of successful military operations carried to "victory": followed by peace terms either imposed or negotiated. But nuclear technology now has forced political leaders to think in terms of an ultimate limit to warfare. The United States saw the point comparatively early. Just after World War II we offered to contribute our atomic monopoly to the United Nations. The offer was rejected, and the Soviets went ahead to develop their bomb. From then on, restraint had to be the product not of multilateral management but of bilateral balance. Today, between the Russians and ourselves, war is restrained by a reciprocal prudence to a limit short of mutual suicide.

Short of that ultimate prudence, Soviet behavior during the past two decades has frequently been erratic. The emplacement of Soviet missiles in Cuba was the most dangerous example, but there have been others. During the 1950s Khrushchev used to threaten to incinerate the orange groves of Italy or to reduce the Acropolis in Athens to radioactive ash. These threats were so clearly disproportionate to known Soviet aims and motives in Europe that the attempted blackmail did not work; if anything, it bound the threatened nations more closely to their Western allies. Three times, Soviet threats to choke off Berlin almost boiled over into war. Each time the Soviet leaders of the day relearned in time the first principle of great-power politics: you had better not bluff unless you mean it, and you had better not mean it if it leads to mutual suicide.

During the early 1960s, both Berlin and Cuba provided a highly educational real-life crisis "game" (to a participant, it did not feel like a game at the time), in which the fear on each side was of almost instant escalation from no fighting at all to fighting with intercontinental weapons. In both cases, the first and effective American riposte was a show of determination at a believable level of violence: reinforcement of the Berlin garrison by a brigade of about 5,000 American troops, a blockade by 90 U.S. warships on the approaches to Cuba and a concentration of air power in Florida—backed up by a partial mobilization of much larger conventional forces and a well-advertised call-up of reserves. In both cases the Soviet thrust was withdrawn before anything but latent violence had to be used, yet nuclear retaliation was the ultimate threat implied by that gentle first step onto the escalator. Because they could not afford to bet that President Kennedy did not mean it, the Soviets backed away; it took them the better part of a year to do so in the 1961–62 Berlin crisis, but only six days in Cuba in the autumn of 1962.

The contrasting case is Vietnam. For many reasons not germane to our argument here, neither Hanoi nor its Soviet backers believed that the steps we took to end the Vietnam war by escalation were likely to result in further steps beyond Hanoi's capacity (with large Soviet aid) to match. That analysis was correct, and President Johnson's Vietnam policy stubbed its toe on the strategic boulder already scarred by Khrushchev's boot. A government, especially a democratic government, cannot imply that more drastic actions will follow unless it is quite clear to the adversary that the country making the threat has the will to follow through. The North Vietnamese and their Soviet advisers saw through the thoughtless Gulf of Tonkin resolution, proposed as it was by a President running for re-election and passed by a mesmerized and emotional Senate. They perceived beyond our government's tough actions a disturbed and thoughtful nation in which internal divisions would probably limit the escalation to (from Hanoi's viewpoint) manageable levels. No one will ever know how they would have reacted if the realistic alternative to capitulation had been nuclear obliteration because nobody can imagine, even in retrospect, that American political leaders would have permitted themselves, or been permitted, to "mean it."

The newer nuclear-weapons states have not yet learned how clumsy, how grotesquely inapplicable to the day-to-day issues of international politics, is the overt and incredible threat to blow one's neighbors to smithereens. The Chinese communists, for example, still seem to have great hopes for nuclear weapons as an index of influence. They will find, I think, that this illusion was just another symptom of underdevelopment. General de Gaulle, too, insisted on building an "independent" nuclear *force de dissuasion*, the fate of which is still uncertain in post-de Gaulle yet Gaullist France. The French nuclear force was already politically vulnerable even in de Gaulle's time; the Frenchman on the street could easily see what trouble the experts had in explaining the circumstances in which it might be used. I once heard a French official explain to Secretary Rusk that the French nuclear weapons would be available to "trigger" a U.S. nuclear response if the Americans seemed reluctant to come to the aid of Western Europe in an emergency. The Secretary inquired politely how that would work. The Frenchman said that if France were poised to send missiles toward Russia, then the Russians would either have to stop their aggression or launch a nuclear attack on NATO, which would automatically involve the United States. "No," said Mr. Rusk thoughtfully, "I think our first reaction would be to make sure the Russians knew where your missiles were coming from."

At the strategic, intercontinental, thermonuclear level, the lesson of Soviet and American experience is clear: the forms of military power that cannot be used in reality cannot be used for blackmail either. President Kennedy once asked in exasperation, "What are my big bombs going to do to solve *that* problem?" There is no doubt that a thermonuclear warhead is a status symbol of enormous significance; but nobody has yet found a way to cash it in for usable diplomatic poker chips.

*　　　*　　　*

Because the superpower stand-off is so clear and the drawbacks of mutual suicide so readily perceived, "deterrence" is often taken as the automatic consequence of possessing strategic nuclear weapons—Polaris submarines prowling the oceans undetected and big Minuteman missiles poised underground in midcontinent U.S.A. But Polaris and Minuteman are only one end of a continuum that also includes tactical nuclear weapons, conventional arms, logistical systems, reinforcements, mobilization plans, command-and-control communications, and above all soldiers, sailors, airmen, and marines. To think straight about defense planning in Europe and the seas around Europe, we can lay aside the mumbo-jumbo of strategic arithmetic, skip the numerology of megatons and megadeaths, and define deterrence as peacekeeping by threat of unacceptable consequences—the use of latent military power, all kinds of military power, in the service of political persuasion.

A responsible leader contemplating military force for the "continuation of political relations . . . by other means" must think through the consequences of his first action. From much practice with long-range planning and war-gaming, and perhaps chess-playing, he has to have learned to recognize the crossroad where logic and politics meet. As the French say it, *il faut vouloir les consequences de ce qu' on veut*—you must not only want what you want, you must also want what it leads to. Deterrence is a Soviet planner unable honestly to tell his political bosses that if they start a military action in Europe for a limited purpose (say, pinching off Berlin, or seizing the Turkish Straits), there is a sure way to keep the resulting fracas limited. In other parts of the world there is a certain experience in keeping limited wars limited. Whatever else may be said of the methods and motivations of fighting in Korea, Vietnam, Borneo, Cuba, Cyprus, Sinai, Goa, and the Rann of Cutch, it has been characterized by severe and conscious limitations by both aggressors and defenders however defined. But in Europe, no one knows whether the escalator of war is similarly self-limiting, because any violence brings nations to the threshold of nuclear war.

Europe has been the most peaceful of postwar continents precisely because neither of the two nuclear superpowers can avoid direct and immediate involvement if a rash move is made there by the other. In Europe, by firm if tacit agreement, the Soviet Union and the United States of America are so deeply committed that they cooperate at arm's length to keep the peace.

It is a grotesque way to accomplish so desirable an object. The European stalemate is expensive, technologically unstable, precarious, enervating, and unpopular. Brezhnev, Senator Mike Mansfield, and the Pope can all agree that the cold war is (as Khrushchev said of Berlin) a bone in the throat. But the stalemate works until something better is invented and agreed on both sides of those ugly walls and barbed-wire barricades. It works because neither side knows how or when the other would first use or react to the use of nuclear weapons. Both sides have enough force to counter any given conventional military move with other conventional moves that give time for careful thought about the use of nuclear weapons. Without the *certainty* that limited force would be met at least with a major delaying action, the temptation to solve problems "surgically" (that was the word used by advocates of bombing Cuba in 1962 and Hanoi in 1967) might be too much to resist: if bluster and a little muscle-flexing can win the argument, why bother to negotiate? Without the *uncertainty* about the use of nuclear weapons, one government or the other might be lured by a clear superiority in conventional armament to try force even if it entailed a few days' fighting.

As long as the Russians continue to invest an impressive proportion of their entire budget in the most modern machinery of war, political majorities in Europe and America have felt obliged to assume that the only sure restraint on the Soviet leaders is their continuing conviction that recourse to armed militancy runs the risk of setting in motion an escalator beyond their control. In short, we think we are deterring the Soviet Union by making sure force will be met by force, and by leaving open how and when—but not whether—nuclear weapons would if necessary be brought into play.

The dilemma of deterrence, then, is how to mix our knowledge of what a potential enemy could do with our judgment about what he would really do. A deterrent force is partly a quantitative function of the adversary's capabilities; but it also reflects a qualitative guess about his intentions. At budget time in each Western government, the advocates of more military spending can be counted on to say that the Soviet Union's capacity to wage war is known, has taken years to develop, will take years to change. This is broadly true, as is the companion claim that the intention of Soviet political leaders is unknown, and can in any event change overnight. But rational as this analysis is, neither the United States nor any of its allies use it as the basis for political judgments about how much to spend on the common defense, how common the defense should be, or what kinds of defense to buy. Whatever their leaders may say to congressional and parliamentary budget committees, the tax-conscious, welfare-minded peoples of the Western democracies have been convinced for a long time that the Soviet Union is not about to pounce on them. That judgment has indeed been proven correct for twenty years, and seems a good prediction for the foreseeable future.

In these circumstances the task of the Western Alliance is not to match the military might of the Warsaw Pact but to be in a position to bring to bear, within the warning time likely to be available, the men and equipment and ammunition and stocks sufficient to prevent Soviet leaders from calculating that resort to any level of armed conflict would be clearly advantageous. This does not mean forces clearly capable of pushing an aggressor back to where he came from. It means enough force to make sure of a tough fight at whatever level of violence the aggressor selects, plus the capacity and willingness to escalate into kinds of warfare that are so unpredictable as to make the very outcome enormously dangerous.

The situation as we move into the 1970s is that Soviet leaders faced by the NATO deterrent (conventional forces in place, tactical nuclear weapons stored in Europe, strategic nuclear weapons at the ready outside of Europe) cannot gamble confidently on the formula, "Heads I win, tails you lose." Neither, of course, can the leaders of NATO. In the toss-up of nuclear destiny, the most optimistic aggressor can hardly predict a better outcome than, "Heads I win, tails we both lose." The Soviet leaders' uncertainty about NATO's response combined with their knowledge of its capacities is the Western deterrent.

*　　　*　　　*

Just as new technology can change the ultimate balance of strategic forces, so research and development can change the very nature of the escalator to nuclear war. In the 1950s, while the doctrine of instant massive retaliation was still our chief reliance, the United States had begun to develop a wide variety of weapons intended for use in more limited nuclear engagements: smaller bombs which could take out an airfield without devastating a country; battlefield artillery designed for use against troop concentrations; nuclear anti-aircraft weapons and atomic demolition devices designed for use over or on the defender's own territory; and a variety of naval nuclear weapons for use against submarines, individual ships, or a whole convoy.

How has this more diversified nuclear arsenal affected the number and pitch of the steps on the escalator? Aside from the obvious logistical efficiency of such weapons, the improved firepower and destructiveness, what do they really mean to the political decision-maker?

I will pause here for a moment to confuse a term which might otherwise acquire a deceptively precise meaning: What is a "tactical nuclear weapon"? The amateur, listening to the professionals talk about these mysteries, is bound to assume that they know the difference between strategic and tactical weapons. But the more he associates with the professionals, the fuzzier become the distinctions he thought were so clear. The Pentagon has been wrestling with this one for a decade.

Sometimes the difference between "strategic" and "tactical" is taken to be a difference in size. There are now nuclear weapons that can make an explosion hardly larger than a sizable conventional bomb. But many of the tactical nuclear weapons are small only by the grotesque standard of a megaton. Secretary McNamara once remarked that we had the equivalent of "5,000 Hiroshimas" stored in West Germany alone. To the strategist these weapons may be relatively small, but to the target, and to the user who draws a retaliation in kind, they would suddenly seem much too big if they ever had to be used.

It is clear enough that an intercontinental missile capable of carrying several megaton warheads is a strategic weapon. It is equally clear that a demolition charge or a short-range anti-aircraft system is a tactical weapon, usable only in local situations or over the defender's territory. But most of the range of weaponry in between is strategic or tactical, depending on who uses it for what against whom.

As we developed nuclear weapons of increasing accuracy and smaller yield, it began to appear that the West was developing the option of countering conventional aggression with a limited nuclear riposte, thus avoiding the dilemma of the Dulles policy— either to quit or to escalate immediately and directly from conventional arms to the use of big long-range nuclear weapons. It was to exploit this enormous advantage that the United States decided to build theater nuclear forces on the continent of Europe. About 7,200 such weapons have now been stockpiled in Europe, but still in American custody, for use of our own and allied ground and air forces in seven countries; and more are available for use by ships of our NATO-committed Atlantic and Mediterranean fleets.

The Soviets are bound to be in a quandary as to what we propose to do with these weapons; their uncertainty is soundly rooted in our own. But it obviously would not do for us to be so uncertain about nuclear planning as to give the Soviets the idea that armed militancy might pay after all.

The difficulty with planning for nuclear war is that there has never been one. We have dropped two primitive bombs, destroying two cities, but we have never been in a "nuclear war." There is no doubt this lack of experience is an unalloyed blessing. Yet the absence of practical experience means there is no such thing as an "expert" on nuclear planning who has acquired his expertise by doing something; he is inevitably forced to resort to theory and extrapolation.

Generals and admirals have qualified as experts in other modes of warfare by studying and practicing a rich inheritance of military wisdom; political leaders are accustomed to the "win, lose, or withdraw" options in war. But the explosive power of modern weapons does not seem to be just another stage in the historical escalation of firepower from the throwing arm to the catapult to the bow-and-arrow to gunpowder. It is a new kind of power. There is much brilliant academic theorizing, but nobody really knows what effect nuclear weapons would have on target troops, on target populations, on the troops using them, and above all on political leaders and governments. In an environment of nuclear blast, fire, and fallout, it is not easy to find real-world referents for trusty concepts like "win" or "lose"—or even "withdraw."

There has indeed been so little experience in making decisions about nuclear weapons that some military leaders profess to think the political decision about the use of nuclear weapons would take place only once—at the beginning—after which it would be left to the military commanders to decide which weapons to use on what targets, in what order, and for how long. But "You may fire when ready, Gridley" will never be said in a nuclear engagement. More likely, unless the total situation were catastrophic, the use of each weapon or group of weapons would be carefully planned by political leaders. The military and political effects of the first weapons would be carefully analyzed by political leaders before any other nuclear weapons were used. Even the smallest and the most "tactical" weapons would be handled with kid gloves by the very highest authorities on both sides of the battle.

We placed in Europe 7,200 of these weapons no one quite

knows how to use because we had them first. The period of tactical nuclear monopoly, however, lasted no longer than the strategic nuclear monopoly endured—four or five years at most. The Soviets have likewise developed "smaller" nuclear weapons (a good deal larger than ours on the average); they have also achieved great accuracy and built a variety of "local" delivery systems. So today the classic model of conventional aggression arrested by tactical nuclear weapons is blurred for the war-gamers by the prospect that NATO's use of tactical weapons could be more or less matched by Soviet forces without the Soviets having to choose further escalation to the big intercontinental missiles.

Under present circumstances, the Soviet leaders' uncertainties about nuclear escalation must persuade them that a large-scale attack on Western Europe, if they have ever seriously considered it, is simply not in the cards. But they do have the capacity for more limited operations—in Berlin or in the eastern Mediter-ranean area, and to a growing extent at sea—and Eastern European allies have forces that could help mount a quick limited action.

NATO must therefore have the capacity to respond, fast and flexibly, to limited military action. Only if it does, will that Soviet military planner have to admit to his political bosses that he cannot guarantee success without the risk of nuclear escalation. Without this capacity, the deterrent applies only to the least likely kinds of emergencies—i.e., the all-out missile strike at the United States or the all-out land assault on Western Europe— and will not deter the more likely forms of military action, or political demands reinforced by military preparations, at the other end of the spectrum.

The crux of deterrence, then, is an assured response of un-certain dimensions. Security of the West demands that the NATO allies persuade the Soviets that armed militancy might lead to the first use by NATO of tactical nuclear weapons, with indeter-minate further escalation to follow.

Chapter IV

The Sharing of Nuclear Uncertainty

As concepts and technology change, the constant in Atlantic nuclear relations is that the United States has the nuclear power and the other allies do not. The British concede that their nuclear capacity is not an independent factor in NATO's equation but a tag end of the U.S. deterrent. The fate of the French program, delayed by the decision to go it alone, is similarly in doubt. Canada is a junior partner in North American defenses, but has had no taste for becoming a nuclear-weapons state. The Federal Republic of Germany is committed to remain a state without nuclear weapons; that was a key part of the package of agreements by which the West Germans joined NATO in 1954. The problem of Atlantic "nuclear sharing" is therefore how all the other allies (or such of them as are interested) can share the U.S. discretion which is reserved by Act of Congress to the President of the United States.

For a dozen years NATO's ugliest arguments about consultation focussed on European complaints about "nuclear sharing." It had long been true that NATO's nuclear strategy was, in practice, worked out unilaterally by the United States government. As long as the doctrine was instant and massive retaliation, the complaints took the form of frequent demands for reassurance that the Americans really meant to strike right away and would not wait to liberate a Europe already overrun.

The worst thing that can happen to a national politician is for his constituents to learn from abroad, rather than from him, what dispositions have been made for their survival. Yet the European public was regularly learning from censored congressional testimony and public speeches by American political leaders just how and when and with what they were to be defended by their distant ally from their nearby adversary. Even the formal announcement of "flexible response" as the philosophy of the Kennedy administration broke in the American press before it was taken up privately in the North Atlantic Council.

For a dozen years, in the 1950s and early 1960s, there was resentment and controversy about "nuclear sharing," and a number of half-measures were taken to palliate it. We allowed some allied officers from SHAPE to sit in the Pentagon and at the Omaha headquarters of the Strategic Air Command; but the officers were junior, and their connection with targeting decisions was more symbolic than real. We assigned three Polaris submarines to the Mediterranean, under command of the Supreme Allied Commander, Europe (SACEUR), to point missiles at Soviet missiles pointed at Western Europe—again an exercise in symbolism since the U.S. target plans had covered those targets anyway. We agreed at Athens in 1962 to "guidelines" about nuclear consultation, and then resisted agreement on procedures to carry them into practical effect. We placed tactical nuclear weapons in half a dozen countries, and trained the forces of seven allies in their use. But we did not share with the Alliance even the bare facts about that stockpile of weapons let alone the rationale that had led us to invent, procure, and deploy them.

Until the mid-1960s, therefore, it is fair to say that we not only failed to consult, we were not even very good about telling our allies about plans made on their behalf to protect their national existence. The Kremlin, which invests a good deal more than our NATO allies do in independent efforts to learn the facts, probably had a more accurate idea than any continental European nation of the extent and disposition of our nuclear forces. If the Soviets did not know how these forces might be used in an emergency, that was because the United States government was not quite sure either.

The most spectacular and least successful effort to resolve the nuclear sharing dilemma was the proposed idea that one nuclear weapons system should be internationally owned and operated—a Multilateral Force, which came to be known as MLF. The least spectacular and most successful such effort was the idea of intensive policy consultation among the interested allies, as practiced now in the Nuclear Planning Group, or NPG. The contrasting stories are instructive, which will lead us to some speculations on the next major bargain in the nuclear field—the effort to agree with the Soviets on the limitation of strategic offensive and defensive systems.

*   *   *

The standard version of the MLF story has it that a small cabal, based in the Department of State, promoted the notion of a mixed-manned nuclear fleet against the combined opposition of the Pentagon, the White House, and the Congress, and tried without success to generate a spark of interest in an apathetic Europe that showed no great interest in financing its own defense anyway. The facts are more complex, and less supportive of the conspiracy theory of history.

The motivation for a Multilateral Force was both relevant and reasonable: "the Europeans," meaning especially the Germans, would in time insist on sharing in some practical way in nuclear decisions heretofore made exclusively by the United States. Failing some resolution of this issue, many thoughtful people on both sides of the Atlantic predicted that "the Europeans" would develop their own weapons, make a hash of the hopes for nuclear non-proliferation, and break up the North Atlantic Alliance.

MLF did originate in the Department of State, as a notion that some one strategic nuclear weapons system should be owned and operated collectively by a group of NATO allies. The warheads would still be controlled by the United States, but the weapons system would be mixed-manned in a rigorously international way. One idea was to internationalize some Polaris submarines—some of ours, plus those which we were helping the British buy and arm (pursuant to the 1962 Nassau bargain, after we had torpedoed a U.S.-U.K. project to develop the Skybolt missile). But the Polaris idea was quickly dropped when Vice Admiral Hyman Rickover, the peppery parent of the nuclear submarine, generated congressional objections on security grounds: foreigners should not get that close to the still-secret design features of our nuclear propulsion device.

The project ultimately proposed was a fleet of surface ships converted to carry strategic missiles with ranges at least sufficient to knock out Soviet medium and intermediate-range missiles threatening the airfields and cities of Western Europe. These ships would be mix-manned, with the commands divided or rotated among the participating nations. Places would be made for sailors, engineers, weapons technicians, and even cooks from any NATO nation choosing to participate. Complicated but ingenious ways were devised to ensure a reasonable efficiency in these unusual circumstances and to safeguard against the contingency that the officers of some nations might want to hold fire while other were anxious to shoot. The entrance fee would have been quite large; unlike most of other NATO nuclear arrangements, where the United States pays the piper while calling the tune, the MLF participants would have had to share the full cost.

An enormous amount of staffwork was done by the Navy, the State and Defense Departments, the Atomic Energy Commission, and the U.S. Mission to NATO; the later stages of the planning were the subject of frequent discussions by a group of eight nations, meeting at NATO headquarters but not as a NATO body to avoid the French objection that awaited any formal proposal along these lines in the North Atlantic Council. This group spelled out how the system would work, how mixed-manning would be managed, how crews could be paid equitably (when some U.S. seamen drew more than some allied captains), how the seemingly multiple fingers on the trigger would be unified, how the ships would be financed, provisioned, governed, and commanded. Such serious, concentrated and professional thought has never, before or since, been devoted to devising supranational arrangements for a modern weapons system. The MLF's intellectual legacy may come in handy some day when bold experiments in international cooperation are in vogue again.

But meanwhile the debate outside the planning offices was raging. Much of the debate picked flaws in the detailed plans. Mixed-manning was used for a time as a swearword on Capitol Hill. Jokes and cartoons about dietary differences and linguistic confusion helped bring the project down. (Problems like these would not in practice have been so troublesome: a cruise by a mixed-manned ship, the U.S.S. *Ricketts*, later demonstrated that mixed-manning could work.) Also contributing to MLF's demise was the general impression that a small group of American true believers in European integration was trying to put something over on every one else; that impression was deepened by the absence of notable enthusiasm in Washington at the Cabinet level or in the White House.

The real trouble with the MLF, however, was that it did not scratch the real itch, merely diverting attention from the wider issue of nuclear sharing for a time. At least three fatal flaws would have killed it even if its public relations had been ideal: the defense of the West did not require yet another strategic missile system; MLF did nothing to cut the Europeans in on the central decisions about nuclear strategy and possible use; and therefore no government was really behind the scheme.

By the mid-1960s, it was common public knowledge that the United States had several times more strategic nuclear explosive power than it could conceivably need for the "assured destruction" of the Soviet Union, even on the wildest sort of assumptions about Soviet science, development, and political behavior. Why, then, should the United States spend more tax money to add more overkill? And why would the Germans, whose postwar prosperity had not been achieved by profligacy, spend good hard Deutschemarks to buy a small tail on a strategic watchdog that already protects them as much as they can be protected in a dangerous world?

The reply from the MLF planners was that the Federal Republic of Germany and other European participants would be buying a voice in nuclear decision-making. But the Europeans could not help noticing that the President of the United States was still required by the McMahon Act to retain the final say on firing the nuclear warheads no matter how many other nations are in the act. The Europeans kept asking, Does the United States propose to keep its finger on the safety catch? The honest answer had to be Yes. It therefore did not stand to reason that the MLF's weapons would ever be fired except as part of a general nuclear strike by the Strategic Air Command and the U.S. Polaris fleet.

Buying into the MLF did not necessarily purchase a seat at the table where *that* decision would be discussed; ownership of some missiles afloat was also quite irrelevant to decisions about deployment and use of the tactical weapons just then being moved to Europe. The Americans argued that common owner-ship of a nuclear fleet would lead naturally to a broad consulting relationship among the owners, covering wider issues of nuclear strategy. But the more skeptical Europeans still wondered whether MLF was a gimmick to divert them from raising the really important and interesting questions about allied nuclear policy.

For these general reasons, and a good many local ones besides, no government was pushing the MLF. The European govern-ments were worried about their own Left pacifists, who objected on principle to involvement with these immoral instruments of war .The more astute politicians were apprehensive also that the United States might not itself stick by its proposal: the em-barrassingly unilateral cancellation of Skybolt was still a fresh political memory, especially in Britain. Some governments, notably the German, Dutch, and Italian, tolerated intensive joint planning for an MLF because it twice appeared, first in the Kennedy and then in the Johnson administration, that the United States really wanted to breathe some life into the project; but no European government would take the "initiative" both American Presidents said they were waiting for.

In retrospect it is clear that George Ball's visit to Bonn in January of 1963, which temporarily persuaded the Adenauer government; the creative policy proposals of Henry Owen in the State Department; the impressive planning efforts of Gerard Smith and Vice Admiral John Lee; Livingston Merchant's diplomatic sales mission; and the vigorous and consistent advocacy of Thomas K. Finletter, U.S. Ambassador to NATO from 1961 to 1965, combined to imply a much more dependable American commitment to the proposal than turned out to be deliverable. The Secretaries of State and Defense were not dedicated to the plan; Presidential Assistant McGeorge Bundy, an early MLF supporter, came to believe it was impractical and unwise. Both Presidents started by blessing the sales effort, and drew back when they noticed the congressional flak and the absence of European enthusiasm. In both administrations the anointed U.S. salesmen found, when the crunch came, that their President had kept wide open the option to drop the MLF if it failed to "take."

Kennedy's political biographers are noticeably protective of him on the MLF. They explain that the proposal was sound and logical if the Europeans wanted it badly enough to pay for it; they concede that the President personally set in motion the tactic that convinced the Germans it had strong U.S. backing; but they try to save Kennedy from historians who might blame him for the debacle by citing evidence of his privately expressed reservations on the subject. My own assumption at the time was that the President was trying, as political executives often do, to have it both ways. If the enthusiasts for MLF could bring it off, it might prove a good answer to a really serious problem—the abrasive complaints from our allies about our reluctance to engage in any real nuclear sharing. If in the end MLF did not float, the President could always walk away from it, saying it had always depended for its success on European initiative—thus exposing the diplomatic advocates rather than the Presidency to congressional and journalistic I-told-you-so's.

President Kennedy was killed before the dilemma was resolved; President Johnson inherited both the problem and the tactic. He too started as an advocate of the project, committing himself to support Ambassador Finletter's efforts to get agreement through the *ad hoc* group in Paris, though not engaging the Presidency to help sell it either at home or abroad. By early 1965 he had withdrawn even his internal support. My first task on arrival in Paris in September 1965 was to help set up a "continuing committee" designed never to meet again. MLF was never murdered—no *corpus delicti,* no embarrassing funeral for one-time advocates to attend. It was just quietly forgotten.

*   *   *

The contrasting story is that of the Nuclear Planning Group—an effort to handle the nuclear-sharing issue inside NATO, avoiding common ownership of a single weapons system, and betting instead on better consultation. Instead of mix-manning the hardware, NPG mix-mans the policy.

Secretary of Defense Robert McNamara had tried not to interfere with the efforts to "sell" the MLF, but he had always thought the root of the problem was to enable those allied governments genuinely interested in doing so to learn enough about atomic realities to participate with us in judgments on how to use this unprecedented weaponry for deterrence and defense. In May 1965, with the agreement of Secretary Rusk, he proposed at a NATO meeting that the Alliance establish a five-member "select committee" for this purpose. It was the right idea, but the wrong proposal. The smaller allies promptly took it as an attempt to rule them off the nuclear course. The British were not sure they wanted to bury in a NATO committee their special relationship with the United States on nuclear questions. The Germans remained reticent—pleased at the prospect of being elected (they assumed) to McNamara's small band, but anxious not to seem overly ambitious in nuclear matters. The Italians, unsure whether they would qualify for the inner circle, were reserved. By early fall it looked as though the McNamara initiative might be stillborn too.

There followed a complex and private negotiation among the Permanent Representatives in Paris. The circle was squared by establishing a Special Committee of all the Defense Ministers who wanted to join, which turned out to be ten. This became the holding company for three smaller groups, on crisis management, on communications, and on nuclear planning. A further negotiation narrowed participation in the "nuclear planning working group," which everybody knew was destined to be the center ring of this little circus, to five. The United States and Britain would be members because they had nuclear weapons; France opted out of the whole enterprise; Germany and Italy would be members because they are big countries; and one member would represent the small countries.

The Netherlands had been so vociferous about the rights of small countries that it was generally assumed the fifth nuclear planner would be Dutch; then the Dutch overplayed their hand by insisting on the juridicial equality of all allies and creating such an impasse over the fifth seat that the Defense Ministers had to troop solemnly into a private room to draw lots. In this Byzantine manner Turkey was elected and joined the American, British, German, and Italian Defense Ministers in what the newspapers (though not the U.S. Secretary of Defense) promptly dubbed the "McNamara Committee."

Out of the other two working groups came practical recommendations that led directly to improvements in technique such as the NATO-wide Communications System and the Brussels Situation Center. In the nuclear planning working group, McNamara wisely declared a moratorium on further discussion of procedures and membership, and plunged into consultation on the "gut" issues of nuclear strategy with which Washington's planners were already struggling. His object was to baptize Europe's Defense Ministers, and through them their governments, by total immersion in the dangers and uncertainties of nuclear weaponry. He held their noses to the grindstone through four meetings that year—an enormous investment in preparation, travel time, and patience.

The drive and energy McNamara put into helping Europeans understand and contribute to nuclear strategy often puzzled our allies even while they appreciated his personal services as their professor of defense nucleonics. His own reasons for putting such stress on the NPG were never articulated, but they came through loud and clear. A thorough understanding of the slender potentialities and inherent limitations of nuclear capabilities was necessary not only to make more meaningful the better intelligence and improved communication lines to be provided to our allies and the more specific consultative procedures to be used, but also to avoid fruitless debates and to discover in the dimensions of the nuclear problem the compromises that may have to be struck. These benefits, in turn, were the prerequisites both to having the allies participate directly in major U.S. decisions on nuclear force structure and strategy and to persuading them to acknowledge their real strategic priorities and adjust their forces accordingly.

There was, moreover, another main benefit to the United States of this special kind of consultation: the fact that exposing our own thinking to foreigners would force us to think harder about our own conclusions than had been required to sell them to ourselves.

In the very first meeting of the nuclear planners, in Washington in 1966, McNamara showed he meant business by discussing Soviet strategy and forces so frankly with the Europeans that the U.S. intelligence community, traditionally wary of telling our allies what we know about Soviet weaponry, was visibly restive. In London in April, the group was treated by British Defense Minister Denis Healey to a detailed briefing on a couple of Central European war games in which large areas and millions of people were destroyed in "tactical" warfare with kiloton weapons. McNamara later said he thought the Alliance had advanced further in its nuclear thinking in the Washington and London meetings than at any other time in the five and one-half years he had been in office.

The Europeans, too, were impressed. The Germans and other nuclear "have-nots" had been assuming that Washington would never listen to a government that did not itself have nuclear weapons, and that real influence was inherently limited to the "haves." Such support as the MLF had generated in Europe was based on this assumption. But in the small circle of the "McNamara Committee," the German and Italian and Turkish participants could see that British access to American minds came not so much from the dubiously relevant British nuclear force—obsolete V-bombers and unbuilt Polaris submarines—as from the fact that Denis Healey, Britain's Secretary of State for Defense, knew what he was talking about and was not bashful about speaking up. They began to see what McGeorge Bundy, still the President's Special Assistant for National Security at the time, said later to a public audience in the United Kingdom:

> . . . the weight of British influence on the test-ban and other nuclear issues has never been significantly affected by the weight of British nuclear forces. . . . British influence has rested on persistence, eloquence, and persuasiveness, not on megatons. An opportunity for similar influence lies open today to any European voice that will take the trouble to study the open record on this perilous subject.

Convinced by midsummer of 1966 that this new nuclear intimacy could be made to work, the members of the "McNamara Committee" agreed at their fall meeting in Rome to recommend a two-tiered set-up: an open-ended Nuclear Defense Affairs Committee which would supposedly hold all the power and do none of the work, and a permanent Nuclear Planning Group to do the work and therefore make allied nuclear policy. Despite the political complications of doing so, the NPG was to be kept as small as possible, to engage the personal participation of Defense Ministers, and to feature extemporaneous discussion of papers read in advance, with a ban on reading papers out loud at the meetings themselves. Both the larger Committee and the nominally subordinate Group would be chaired by the Secretary General, who naturally considered it a point of some importance not to be frozen out of the Alliance's most dynamic consultative forum. McNamara, who had chaired the temporary working group, preferred that Ministers rotate the chair among themselves, but quickly recognized that Brosio's support was a priceless ingredient of the political mix.

McNamara felt especially strongly about keeping the NPG small, which was of course the stickiest part of the bargain. At a background press conference after the Rome meeting he tried to explain his preference for international intimacy:

> . . . The best budget, fellows, is the brick walls of a building. . . . Whenever I want to be really efficient, I get a building about half the size that anybody wants and say that's what we're going to build Ford cars in or that's what we're going to have for the Navy or whatever it may be. Well, we followed the same procedure here and we designed small tables and said that nobody can talk that doesn't

sit at the table and there are only X number of spaces at the table. Now, this sounds childish maybe, but it isn't childish. There's a very direct inverse relationship between the number of participants and the degree or extent of accomplishment.

At the regular December conclave of the Alliance that year (1966), the deed was done. France, Iceland, and Luxembourg stayed off the Nuclear Defense Affairs Committee by their own choice. Of the remaining twelve, Portugal and Norway decided, for the time being, not to join the nominally subordinate Nuclear Planning Group. That Group had to be expanded to seven to accommodate the ambitions of the remaining ten, and even so two classes of membership had to be established. In the end permanent seats were given to Britain, Germany, Italy, and the United States; Greece and Turkey alternated in a fifth seat; and two more seats were shared by the remaining four, Canada and The Netherlands for the first eighteen months, then Denmark and Belgium for the same period. For the period after January 1, 1970, this "gentlemen's agreement" would be open to revision. By the time the Turks, Canadians, and Dutch rotated off the NPG they had developed such a lively interest in the work that they attended as "alumni" when the Group met (which by then was most of the time) at the level of NATO Ambassadors. The meetings of Defense Ministers continued as a seven-man club.

*   *   *

NPG was designed for the deep study of both "strategic" and "tactical" nuclear forces. On the strategic equation we had done our homework, and had a rationale which was published in the annual "posture statements" by the Secretary of Defense to committees of the U.S. Congress. (One of NPG's early successes was to encourage Ministers to read these documents, which had been in the public domain right along.) Out of the welter of calculations and estimates, it became all too clear that the United States could wreck the Soviet Union, the Soviet Union could wreck the United States (and Western Europe too if need be), and the offense was so far ahead of the defense that nothing could be done about it by either side, except to exercise the utmost restraint to avoid what McNamara frankly called "mutual suicide."

The first and easiest conclusion of the original McNamara Committee was therefore McNamara's own conclusion: that the nuclear forces the United States already had produced and programmed were adequate to deter large-scale attack, but that there seemed to be no way to prevent unacceptable damage to the West from an all-out nuclear exchange. Instant and massive retaliation was thus formally buried. But then the Europeans began to read in their newspapers about the burgeoning American debate about whether to deploy an antiballistic missile (ABM) system to protect this American force which the Americans had just declared unprotectable. Harder questions began to be asked.

The game of deterrence is played on the terrain of the adversary's assumptions and psychology, and a sophisticated game it is. Already in magazine interviews and press seminars, McNamara had publicly suggested the paradox. The United States would be more secure, he said, after the Soviets hardened their missiles, than it was while their missiles were highly vulnerable to attack. Our fear was that they might fear that we were about to attack their unprotected but formidable missiles, and in a condition of high political tension might be tempted to launch their missiles before the Americans could get to them. Whereas if their force had been hardened and therefore was less vulnerable, the Soviets would be correspondingly more willing to hold their fire in the absence of actual attack.

Now, he explained, we think the Chinese in the mid-1970s will be in a situation analogous to that of the Soviets in the early 1960s—they will have some big intercontinental missiles able to reach the United States, or Western Europe for that matter, but they will still be highly vulnerable if caught in their silos. Therefore, if there were to be tension between the Chinese and the United States, or between the Chinese and the West as a whole, the Chinese might be tempted to launch, believing that we were going to launch against them and wanting to avoid the destruction of their force. Superiority in offensive missiles does not protect us against that contingency, but an antiballistic missile system might; if it could, it ought to be built and deployed.

For Europeans accustomed to a narrower focus and less apocalyptic weaponry, this was heady stuff. But it suggested another question: If it is worthwhile for the United States to have an ABM umbrella, should Western Europe insist on having one too? Certainly it was an unattractive prospect to see both the U.S. and the U.S.S.R. building defense systems, while leaving Western Europe naked.

These issues generated a more serious transatlantic fracas than was really necessary, because of an accident of American timing. McNamara had a long-scheduled date for a speech in San Francisco a week before he was to meet with the Nuclear Planning Group in Ankara at the end of September 1967. Despite predictions that the allies would not appreciate it, he decided to announce the "anti-Chinese" sentinel system in the San Francisco speech—which, except for that announcement, was in effect an argument in favor of settling for parity with the Soviet Union. Unfortunately for the logic of his case, he explicitly held open the possibility of going beyond the anti-Chinese rationale to protect some of our Minuteman missile sites, which seemed to contradict his own argument that the Russians could readily saturate any ABM system we yet knew how to invent, and we could do the same to theirs.

The effect on his fellow-Defense Ministers was electric. When McNamara arrived in Ankara, Denis Healey led the charge in private, and later in public. But curiously, the U.S. government did not, by bypassing its own nuclear consultation forum, wound it beyond repair. The ABM issue gave the Europeans the first major occasion to tangle with the redoubtable McNamara, and they found it did not wreck the Alliance for them to do so. McNamara even retreated a little under fire: protecting the Minuteman had not really been decided yet, he told the press afterwards, and European views would be taken into account before that decision was made.

If it had not been for the hassle about the timing of the San Francisco announcement, the NPG nations would probably have been ready to say in 1967 that ABMs were not for Europe. That, however, would have looked like automatic endorsement of an American line, so they decided instead to look further into how Europe might be protected in the missile age. The following spring they agreed without difficulty that no European ABM system could catch enough incoming Russian missiles to make a difference (the technical problem is even more difficult than in the U.S. case, because of the shorter times involved), and the Americans could worry on their own about the Chinese threat.

A year later the Nixon administration changed the rationale again, featuring just that part of the package which Healey and others had thought least defensible in the Johnson era. But by then the atmosphere was different. No European seriously thought Europe could afford any kind of an ABM system; and President Nixon, though he did not consult ahead of time, personally briefed the NATO Ministers at the Twentieth Anniversary Meeting of the North Atlantic Council. In 1969, ABM was the symbol of an epic battle in U.S. domestic politics, and our allies knew they were just looking on from the outside.

*   *   *

The April 1966 meeting of the McNamara Committee in London, had begun to delve deeply into the dilemmas of deterrence by nuclear escalation. By the time NPG began its official existence in early 1967, the focus of its work was already charted: it would launch the first international inquiry into the usability of tactical nuclear weapons. Considering that these weapons cost hundreds of thousands of dollars apiece on the average, that the stockpile in Europe reached 7,200 before "sufficiency" was declared, and that seven of the allies (Belgium, Canada, Germany, Greece, Italy, The Netherlands, and Turkey) were training forces to use some of them in case of need, it was none too soon for the Alliance to consider when and under what conditions that need might arise, and just how the allies would consult each other if it did. The first conclusion—that, as with strategic weapons, there seemed to be quite enough tactical weapons at hand—was quick and easy. After that, the questions got harder at an exponential rate.

Some European war-gamers, in trying to think through what a localized nuclear engagement would be like, had uncomfortably concluded that most of the destruction would take place on NATO territory. They were almost bound to assume for purposes of a "game" that aggression starts from the East, that the invader starts with conventional weapons, and that he is successful enough (that is, penetrates deeply enough into NATO territory) to cause the allies to make the excruciating decision to use tactical nuclear weapons to fulfill their mutual Treaty commitment.

If both sides were trying to prevent a further escalation to near-total mutual destruction, they might then try to restrict the use of tactical weapons to the battlefield area. But the battlefield area is by definition Western Europe, perhaps Western Germany for the most part. And when the planners began to calculate the effects of several hundred or even several dozen nuclear explosions—"small" by modern standards but still averaging something like the Hiroshima bomb—the conclusion was inescapable that a sizable segment of Western Europe and millions of lives would be the price of stalemating the aggression and persuading the aggressor to think again.

Then, too, if limited nuclear warfare were expanded to the territory of enemy countries, one could expect as a minimum the extension of destruction to most of Western Europe. Sober political leaders in some NATO countries—not only the peace-minded Nordics but well-informed British and German leaders too—had therefore been inclined to say that they could hardly visualize a situation in which it would be clearly advantageous for NATO to be the first to use nuclear weapons.

Yet here was serious danger for the whole strategy of deterrence. A strategy of managed escalation requires a Western willingness to go first, as President Kennedy had recognized (in his talk with General de Gaulle) as early as 1961. If the Soviets were to become convinced that the Western allies could not seriously contemplate recourse to theater nuclear force, even if NATO were losing a conventional war, the uncertainty in Russian minds, which is the deterrent in Europe, could be gradually replaced by a conviction that the West would never cross the threshold from conventional to nuclear war. And if a future Khrushchev seriously believed this, he might well try to pinch off Berlin or make some other limited gain by a quick thrust designed to present NATO with the choice of accepting an accomplished fact or starting a bigger war.

Not all the cases are as touchy as the battlefield weapons. A "demonstration" shot could be exploded in such a way as to avoid mass destruction; that would be the least difficult nuclear decision to make, but it might also serve only to demonstrate the demonstrator's reluctance to use nuclear weapons. Some tactical weapons are clearly defensive. There are atomic demolition munitions that can make a bigger mess of a larger acreage than any conventional charge, and are inherently usable only on territory the using nation owns or controls—for example, to blow up a defile in the mountains through which an invading force would like to come. There are anti-aircraft weapons—the Nike-Hercules system is deployed in Europe—which again make possible a nuclear "first-use" over one's own territory. There are also weapons for use at sea, where the distance from innocent bystanders might be such as to make them usable without hitting what you do not want to hit, without significant fallout, and without necessarily drawing retaliation in kind. Even a two-sided war at sea is arguably less escalatory than explosions of similar yield on populated land would be.

After a year in clearing this kind of intellectual underbrush, Denis Healey and the German Defense Minister, Gerhard Schroeder, volunteered to draft some guidelines for the use of tactical nuclear weapons. This first major effort under European leadership became the centerpiece of NPG's work program. As the work on guidelines proceeds, it increasingly brings into public discussion a basic dilemma. It is natural for Europeans to feel that if conventional defense fails in Europe, the use of nuclear weapons by NATO should rapidly escalate to a strategic exchange between the U.S. and Russia, leaving Europe comparatively intact. It is natural for Americans to press for effective, which is to say large-scale, use of nuclear weapons on the battlefield—

enough to "stop the enemy in his tracks." But this conjures up for Europeans the picture of a Europe devastated while the United States and the Soviet Union remain intact.

The question is of course infinitely postponable, unless a war crisis were to make it suddenly urgent. But even in the fortunately academic discussions of such an issue the positions taken by ministers and ambassadors, no matter how abstractly and hypothetically stated, produce all sorts of political fallout as each tries to divine what the other has in mind, and what responsible governments might really do or fail to do in a real-life emergency.

The growing conviction that the Alliance cannot be certain what it would do to carry out a strategy of uncertainty has naturally turned NATO's attention more and more to the "procedural question." The United States and Britain have repeatedly agreed to consult their allies about the use of nuclear weapons, but no way of doing this in a crisis has ever been agreed. How *does* NATO go to nuclear war?

Anybody who has worked for Presidents of the United States, who have by law the solitary finger on the nuclear button, approaches this question with studied reluctance. Sovereign governments do not and cannot decide ahead of time how they will act or even whom they will consult; that depends on time and circumstance. At every stage of NATO's life as an organization, the smaller countries have quite naturally tried to maximize the influence which their status as allies can bring to bear on the actions of the larger members. The nub of the issue is whether in an emergency some members might act in the name of the Alliance as a whole, even if all had not agreed to do so. By common consent, this constitutional issue is never brought to a head, for there is potential conflict between two NATO dogmas which can both be traced back to the Treaty itself: that NATO actions are taken by unanimous consent, and that "any number can fight." No member can concede in peacetime that its opinion in a life-or-death emergency might be ignored by the others. But neither can any member concede in peacetime that what it decides to do about its NATO obligations might be restrained by the contrary views of its allies. The presumption of cooperation is not *that* strong.

The "procedural question" is therefore unanswerable, and will never be answered except in an emergency, when it counts. As far as nuclear decisions are concerned, my observation is that no one in Europe wants the President to move over and allow other fingers on the button. The answerable question is therefore how governments with relevant views get to the President in time, and how they participate in subsequent judgments about a nuclear situation even after the first use of a nuclear weapon. The most important part of that question is also, by coincidence, the most answerable part: How do governments make sure their views are relevant? They do so by unremitting attention to nuclear problems in peacetime. An ally who knows what he is talking about is an ally most likely to be listened to, even if the time for listening is short. Here is the central purpose of the Nuclear Planning Group, and here precisely is where it is succeeding.

Since so many of the nuclear questions yield to study but not to neat conclusions, the outcomes of nuclear planning are bound to be less significant than the process itself; NPG's main products are its by-products. Thinking deeply about nuclear strategy has increasingly convinced the Germans and other Europeans, as it had earlier convinced the United States during the Kennedy administration, that a flexible response based in the first instance on conventional forces is clearly preferable to immediate resort to nuclear operations of which the nature and outcome are inherently impossible for either side to foresee. And (at least on the nuclear forces in Europe) we are now giving our European allies so much information and creating so many occasions for them to come forward with their ideas, their papers, and their proposals that it is hard for them to feel, let alone complain out loud, that they are not "participating in nuclear planning." Because they are.

*   *   *

The substance of the issues considered in these free, frank, and privileged consultations is extremely complex and as sensitive as any subject dealt with by any government in the world of today.

The inherent divergence of views is, moreover, still quite wide; perhaps it will remain so, since the interests of the transatlantic partners are far from identical. But at least there exists a framework of orderly and informed discussion within which the American government can make known its tentative views before they get too firm, and seek an allied consensus or "no objection," if not full and positive agreement.

There are real dangers here. The relationship between NATO's tactical nuclear forces and the U.S. strategic forces raises broad issues of deterrence policy. There are dangers in surfacing doubts —ours as well as others'—about the usability of tactical nuclear weapons. A general impression that we have serious difficulty in deciding how to use them would erode their value as a key part of the escalator of deterrence. On balance, however, the advantages of continuing to talk with our allies seriously, candidly, and privately through the NPG have been judged by three U.S. Secretaries of Defense, and the administrations they represented, to outweigh the risk of discovering that questions of nuclear strategy have no easy answers. It may even be that the Soviets know that too.

*   *   *

Managing the "up" escalator in wartime is only one side of the transatlantic nuclear-sharing issue. How to manage a "down" escalator in peacetime, through the negotiated limitation and reduction of strategic nuclear systems, is also a central preoccupation of the Western security caucus. Unlike the NPG issues, strategic arms control engages the interests of all fifteen NATO members; even France, which stands aside from formal disarmament talks with the Soviets at Geneva, sits in as an interested party when the North Atlantic Council considers what the Western position in East-West arms talks ought to be.

The postwar history of allied consultations on arms control has followed the pattern of U.S.-Soviet arms control negotiations themselves: desultory in the 1950s, peripheral in the 1960s. But in the 1970s, planning for nuclear arms control may be the liveliest form of "nuclear sharing" in the Alliance.

Throughout the decade of the 1950s, the Soviets made quite an impression around the world by advertising Moscow's desire to achieve general and complete disarmament. In their quieter moments they would concede that a journey of a thousand miles starts with a single step—even if they were unlikely to use so Chinese a way of saying it. But their propaganda machine derived much more nourishment from reiterating the ultimate objective than from discussing the more difficult question of how to start the trip.

For many years the reaction of the Western governments, and especially the United States, was to ridicule proposals for general and complete disarmament as propaganda and to call instead for a discussion of next steps in practical arms control: "open skies," measures against accidental war, a nuclear test ban, a freeze on the production of fissionable materials, and the like. This was of course a sensible position to take, but it was no match in people's aspirations or the news media for the glittering generalities of the Soviet line. (It was also tarnished by our tendency to mention, as examples of practical arms control, measures which would merely stop the other side from doing what we had already done in the field of advanced weaponry. During one period the U.S. government actually refrained from destroying some obsolete medium jet bombers so that they could be contributed to a "bomber bonfire" we were then pushing.)

In conference after international conference, the Soviets bludgeoned the American delegates with speeches on general disarmament, and the Americans had only "next steps" to work with in reply. Then, in the first year of the Kennedy administration, a few officials began to ask the country-boy question, "Why don't we come out for general and complete disarmament, too?" At first it seemed a terribly radical thing to do, and it took some months to get used to the idea that verbal advocacy of Utopia would not unduly endanger the Republic. There was even a last-minute argument in Washington over whether to call the new American policy something distinctive, like "comprehensive and total disarmament." In the end, a pragmatic President approved a declaratory policy favoring general and complete disarmament.

Quite suddenly, the Soviets found that their own drum-beating for the same goal no longer reverberated in world politics as it had done for a decade past. Even neutrals and peace advocates around the world began telling the Soviets that now the goal is agreed, the superpowers should really give some attention to "next steps."

During the 1960s, in consequence, some kind of negotiation about disarmament was in progress nearly all the time. But a NATO preoccupied with its own defense buildup was slow to focus on the reality that planning for arms control was, from the allied point of view, the mirror-image of NATO defense planning.

On the early "non-armament agreements"—the Antarctica Treaty, the Outer Space Treaty, the U.N. ban on bombs in orbit—NATO members typically contented themselves with general exhortations to get on with it. Even the more significant ban on above-ground nuclear testing was remote from the internal politics of most European states; politicians could stir up their local supporters by advocating greater speed or quicker U.S. concessions, but the test-ban negotiation itself was widely regarded as a matter for the nuclear powers—in practice, the United States and Britain, since Gaullist France made its own abstention clear from the outset.

NATO consultation about the Geneva disarmament talks and the early stages of the Non-Proliferation Treaty was similarly half-hearted. Both the Ten-Nation Disarmament Committee (five NATO and five Warsaw Pact nations) and the U.N.-blessed Eighteen-Nation Disarmament Committee (which added eight neutrals) served as a useful polemical safety valve; but every one knew that the marathon Geneva "negotiations" were significant mostly because they provided a respectably multilateral "cover" for continuing bilateral conversations between the American and Soviet co-chairmen, through which we (and our allies at second remove) maintained quite an accurate measure of the U.S.S.R.'s pulse on arms-control issues. When the Geneva talks turned (in 1969) to the idea of an agreement about yet another unarmed environment, this time the seabed, the interest of the North Atlantic Council was engaged because all but one of the allies

is a maritime nation. Even so, more Council time was spent that
season on how to get another NATO member elected to the
Geneva committee than on how to keep weapons of mass destruction off the ocean floor.

Alliance interest in the Non-Proliferation Treaty fell into two
stages, a desultory one and an extremely active one. During the
first stage, which lasted until the winter of 1966–67, the Soviets
were slow to realize their own interest in a treaty by which the
nuclear "have-nots" would forego nuclear weapons and the
"haves" would help keep them that way. During this period verbal
endorsements of nuclear non-proliferation were easy to come by
in Canada and Western Europe. Then suddenly the U.S.-Soviet
talks became serious, and the mood in Europe changed.

Part of the change of mood was due to the way the United
States government started the consultation. The non-proliferation
formula which finally "took," a simple reciprocal promise not
to make, receive, or transfer nuclear weapons, was worked out
bilaterally toward the end of 1966 around the edges of the U.N.
General Assembly in New York. Only several weeks later were
the NATO allies brought up to date. Even those allies which had
been urging greater speed and more concessions to achieve a
treaty were so unhappy about the procedure that they made
difficulties about the substance as a matter of principle.

Yet the long NATO negotiation which then ensued was not all,
or even mostly, the product of procedural pique. That the
Soviets were serious about a treaty was an important new fact in
East-West politics. Each European politician, in office or wishing
to be in office, had to think hard about whether he was willing to
write his signature in indelible ink on a paper which officially
recognized his nation as permanently second-class in the nuclear
age. Especially in Italy and the Federal Republic of Germany,
all sorts of deep and serious reservations came to the surface. No
responsible German wanted to reserve the right to make nuclear
weapons; the Federal Republic had in fact already given up that
right as part of the arrangements by which it became a NATO
ally in 1954. But many responsible Germans argued that the
Soviets would be giving up nothing in signing such a treaty, and

thought it would be better to hold Germany's signature—which the Soviets obviously considered valuable—until the day when it could be traded for something of commensurate political value, such as a reunified Germany in a durable European settlement.

The inspection provisions of the draft treaty, moreover, raised quite difficult problems for the European Six. Having agreed to pool their civil atomic energy efforts in EURATOM, they were worried that a wider inspection agency, the U.N.-related International Atomic Energy Agency, might help the French to destroy the fragile European entity by substituting wider and looser safeguards for EURATOM arrangements already designed to prevent diversion of nuclear materials to military uses.

In the end the treaty was considered word by word and phrase by phrase in the North Atlantic Council. Its political meaning, its inspection provisions, its relationship to an integrated Europe, its constraints on peaceful uses of nuclear energy, and the procedures for reviewing and amending it were active weekly Council agenda items for the better part of a year. As often happens in a supposedly multilateral consultation, much of the real work went on behind the scenes between U.S. and German disarmament officials, and with Italy as well. It was a combination of these detailed explanations and interpretations (negotiated bilaterally and confirmed in the North Atlantic Council), plus the influence of the other allies as expressed through the Council discussions, that brought the treaty close to being signed by Italy and the Federal Republic just before the invasion of Czechoslovakia in August 1968. The Soviet move provided a further reason for delay, on which opponents of the treaty seized with alacrity and skill.

The Non-Proliferation Treaty is by any test a landmark in man's too-gradual adjustment to the implications of nuclear weaponry. The negotiating circus that produced it had many rings—in Moscow, in Washington, in Geneva, at the U.N. in New York, in Vienna, at the offices of the European Commission in Brussels, and in the North Atlantic Council. But without the intensive consultation in NATO there would have been no treaty. That year-long process came to be regarded in NATO as something like the standard of how transatlantic consultation should be conducted—once it got under way.

*   *   *

On his thirty-sixth day in office, President Richard Nixon leaned forward in the United States seat at the North Atlantic Council table in Brussels and made there the most far-reaching commitment to consultation ever offered by any American President to any international organization. He had prepared for this moment by years of personal talks with the leaders of other nations, months of political speeches implying dissatisfaction with what he saw as an American reluctance to take close allies into our confidence, and days of intensive briefings before his European trip. In a carefully considered statement, the President said this to his NATO allies:

> In due course, and with proper preparation, we shall enter into negotiations with the Soviet Union on a wide range of issues, some of which will directly affect our European allies. We will do so on the basis of full consultation and cooperation with our allies, because we recognize that the chances for successful negotiations depend on our unity. . . . I pledge to you today, that in any negotiations directly affecting the interests of the NATO nations, there will be full and genuine consultation before and during those negotiations.
>
> Beyond consulting on those negotiations, and beyond consulting on other policies that directly affect the NATO nations themselves, I intend to consult on a broad range of other matters. I shall not only welcome but actively seek the counsel of America's NATO partners on the questions that may affect the peace and stability of the world in whatever the part of the world in which they arise.

As we left the Council chamber, an awed member of the British delegation to NATO saw the potential in the promise. "My God," he whispered, "*my* government would never make a commitment like that!" But no government, even Britain in its imperial heyday, had ever been called upon to negotiate about the "assured destruction" of its allies. The U.S.-Soviet Strategic Arms Limitation Talks—first nicknamed SALT in dispatches from the U.S. Mission to NATO—involve discussing with NATO's presumed adversary the control or even reduction of the deterrent strength our allies do not have because we did not want them to have it. Small wonder that political leaders in every allied nation regard SALT not as a spectator sport but as business affecting their destiny, which requires the most active possible intramural consultation.

The idea of limiting strategic systems is not new. Ever since Hiroshima the inventors of the bomb, the serious scholars of modern strategy, and political leaders of both the East and West have tormented themselves with public descriptions of the catastrophe to which an arms race with ultimate weapons could lead. Perhaps the most anguished cry was that of Nikita Khrushchev, in his long, rambling, highly personal letter to President Kennedy at the critical moment in the Cuban missile crisis on October 26, 1962. Russian ships were steaming toward the destroyer picket line around Cuba, and Khrushchev was obviously trying to provide a basis for backing away from the confrontation:

> If you have not lost your self-control, and sensibly conceive what this might lead to, then, Mr. President, we and you ought not now to pull on the ends of the rope in which you have tied the knot of war, because the more we pull, the tighter the knot will be tied. And a moment may come when the knot will be tied so tight that even he who tied it will not have the strength to untie it, and then it will be necessary to cut that knot; and what that would mean is not for me to explain to you, because you yourself understand perfectly of what terrible forces our countries dispose.
>
> Consequently, if there is no intention to tighten that knot and thereby doom the world to the catastrophe of thermonuclear war, then let us not only relax the forces pulling on the ends of the rope, let us take measures to untie that knot. We [the leaders of the Soviet Union] are ready for this.

This rare insight into the private anxieties of Soviet leaders confirmed what many American leaders have thought and publicly said: that the Soviet Union and the United States share a crucial interest in turning back the arms race by agreement. Although the correspondence in the 1962 crisis provided a basis for such negotiations, the steps in that direction remained hesitant and mutually suspicious. Some mind-sets on both sides had first to be modified. The Soviets have been obsessed with the achievement of "parity," at least in land-based missiles, and throughout the 1960s they drove with single-minded determination toward that elusive and increasingly expensive goal. At the same time many American leaders were proud of U.S. strategic "superiority" and loath to abandon it as national policy. Throughout the 1960s the U.S. government could and did claim superiority; but even those who made the claim came increasingly to wonder whether the boast was wise, or even likely to remain true.

As NATO's nuclear planners began in 1966 and 1967 to dig into the numerology of nuclear balance, the planned size of the U.S. strategic force was nearly achieved: 1,054 land-based intercontinental ballistic missiles, 41 Polaris submarines with 16 missiles each, and about 650 intercontinental bombers. The scale of Soviet effort to reach nuclear parity (at least in land-based missiles) was not yet known, and McNamara was able in explaining our strategic doctrine to NATO allies to have it both ways: we were "superior," but all we needed was parity anyway.

We were indeed far "ahead" in targetable warheads, which the U.S. government had come to regard as the relevant measure; 3 or 4 to 1 was the public version, and even that ratio probably overestimated Soviet progress at the time. "In part that's an accident," McNamara told the press in a background briefing during a trip to Europe. "It wasn't planned that way. We have always protected against the high end of the threat projection, and therefore we end up at any given time with a greater numerical superiority than we actually planned for that time. . . . To that degree we were wasting some resources. But on the other hand we didn't know how to provide the security we need as an alliance, without buying that extra insurance." The Europeans quickly got the point that both sides have built up forces to a point that far exceeds a credible second-strike capability against the forces each started with—and that is the modern definition of an arms race.

Meanwhile the Soviets were changing the calculus of catastrophe by digging holes and planting large missiles at a rate which would take them past our 1,054 Minutemen very early in the 1970s, and they were building submarines in a hurry too. McGeorge Bundy, looking back in 1969 on the debate about "superiority," drew the frank conclusion: "It is in the nature of the strategic arms race that over time, if two runners are determined and willing to spend, their efforts will tend toward parity. Both the Americans and the Russians are determined and willing to spend. So in the long run a broad parity is inescapable, and the really serious questions are whether it will be stable or unstable in nature, moderate or gigantic in cost."

The mysteries of stability and cost were deepened by two kinds of scientific and technological "progress." The only defense against offensive missiles had been the deterrent presence of other offensive missiles; but now both the Russians and the Americans came to believe they could successfully shoot down at least some of the incoming missiles. Before this potentially good news was even absorbed by the public, the United States let it be known that it had learned how to stuff several multiple independently targeted re-entry vehicles (MIRVs) into a single intercontinental delivery wagon, and that we had to assume the Soviets would in time be able to do likewise. Indeed, they would be able to fit more MIRVs in their missiles because they have more powerful boosters. Decisions to improve our existing systems by making them MIRVs (that is, buying the Minuteman III for land-based systems and the Poseidon missile for the Polaris submarines) combined with decisions to go ahead with the defensive anti-ballistic missile systems (two kinds of missiles and several new varieties of radar, mixed in somewhat different ways by the Johnson and Nixon administrations). The purpose was to ensure that if destabilizing the arms race were the way to stay "ahead," the United States would not be found wanting.

The Soviets, who in 1969 did not seem very sure of their one ABM system around Moscow and did not yet have independently targetable warheads, could be expected to follow suit. But there was a chance that the Soviet leadership would take another look at the knot in which rival technologies were tying both nations, and try negotiation as a substitute for the vast expenditures and appalling uncertainties that predictably lay ahead. President Johnson had earnestly and insistently urged them to join in negotiating the limitation of strategic arms; McNamara had seized the occasion of the summit meeting at Glassboro, New Jersey, to talk directly to Premier Kosygin about getting started.

In the periodic NATO consultation about the talks to limit strategic arms, nobody knew for sure whether the Soviets were likely to be willing to negotiate. It seemed likely that, in the secret recesses of the Kremlin, the Russian leaders were having the same arguments that the President was hearing among the Joint Chiefs of Staff, the Arms Control and Disarmament Agency, the Atomic Energy Commission, the Defense Department, the State Department, the White House staff, and several elements of the congressional leadership. By the summer of 1968 the Soviets had agreed to President Johnson's proposal to negotiate, and a summit meeting to discuss SALT and other issues was set for Leningrad; the announcement of time and place was in fact scheduled for mid-morning of August 21. The evening before, Russian tanks crossed the Czech frontier, and all bets were off— for a time.

It is a measure of the mutual interest in controlling the strategic arms race that the delay was only a little more than a year. At first the Soviets pressed us to negotiate anyway; an impression of business-as-usual would help make their case that the Czech affair had nothing to do with outsiders. President Johnson also tried to keep open, until a few days before he left office, the option of reinstituting a peace-making summit, even though none of the allies thought it good politics or good taste to return so precipitately to negotiations-as-usual with the practitioners of the Brezhnev Doctrine. The President had no interest in doing the Soviets a favor; but he was still deeply impressed with the importance of getting agreement to halt the arms race before it ran beyond the effective control of men and nations.

Once the U.S. election campaign was under way, the idea of a lame-duck summit no longer seemed practical, but there was still sentiment in Washington for starting the talks on strategic arms limitation as soon as possible, in lower key at a lower level. This time our European allies, who had been urging speed before the invasion of Czechoslovakia, urged caution and delay. Let us complete the post-invasion "beefing up" of NATO defenses, they said, before introducing into European relations with the United States the disturbing factor of a major U.S.-U.S.S.R. negotiation.

When he came into office January 1969, President Nixon also

began moving toward the elusive arms-control talks, but with a difference. The difference lay partly in his declaratory policy about Alliance consultation—though the promise to consult with NATO "before and during" any U.S.-U.S.S.R. negotiations only made more explicit the procedure which the Johnson administration had been planning to follow if the missile talks had started the year before. Part of the difference was semantics: the 1968 campaign oratory about the need to maintain strategic "superiority" was muted after seven days in office to a policy of nuclear "sufficiency." The real difference, however, was in the connection to be made between disarmament talks and other U.S.-U.S.S.R. issues.

Presidents Kennedy and Johnson operated essentially on the theory that it was good to be talking with the communists even if nothing tangible came of it for the time being: in the disarmament field, for instance, the Geneva negotiations and U.N. debates were regarded as something of a deterrent in themselves. President Nixon favored a policy of "parallel progress" (journalistically known as "linkage," a term he never used and did not like) embracing both substantive conflicts (such as Vietnam, Laos, and the Arab-Israel war) and arms-control issues. Even if we could get an arms freeze, he would tell visitors, the United States and the Soviet Union would have plenty of arms left to blow up the world; we had better work harder on the issues nations go to war about.

Again there were long delays in setting up the bilateral talks. First the new administration in Washington had to decide that it was ready to negotiate; then, late in the spring of 1969, it seemed that the Soviets had lost their enthusiasm for the project and were searching their souls again. Finally the talks were set for mid-November in Helsinki, Finland, to start between special negotiators, without the overtones of summitry which had complicated the arrangements the year before.

If the Strategic Arms Limitation Talks get going in earnest, they may well continue in one form or another throughout the decade of the 1970s, and perhaps beyond. The negotiators will have to decide what strategic weapons are, how to equate them, and what to include in the equation; they will have to decide whether to start with a partial or total freeze, whether (and how) to restrain new technologies like ABMs and MIRVs, what to do about inspection to keep any bargains honest. They will be looking over their shoulder at China, at Southeast Asia, at the Middle East, at Germany, at the Mediterranean Sea and the oceans beyond, even at outer space and the planets. Only the overriding importance of their work will keep them at it.

On our side of the negotiation, we will presumably be consulting with our North Atlantic allies "before and during" each step of the way. The first requirement for "real" consultation is the U.S. government's willingness to consult before it makes up its own collective mind. But the second requirement is equally important: that our partners in consultation take the process seriously, do their homework assiduously, and state their considered views frankly and openly. In mid-1968, when we were close to a summit meeting on this subject, no NATO government except the United Kingdom had a senior official working fulltime on it. By mid-1969 the staff work in Europe on arms control had improved somewhat, but not nearly enough. If the Alliance becomes a true Western caucus, which the United States can use as a dependable source of relevant advice and consent on nuclear arms limitation, the decisions which the President eventually has to make can serve the interests of our European and Canadian allies too. If the Alliance fails to take this consultation as seriously as the President has said he will take it, "nuclear sharing" could again become the ugliest and most divisive issue in transatlantic politics.

Chapter V

The Western Defense Bargain

When you read in the headlines about a NATO crisis, the chances are that it has to do with how the Alliance partners will, as a key NATO document defines it, "maintain a full spectrum of military capabilities in order to deter and, if necessary, counter aggression." The second half of the 1960s saw three such crises: the withdrawal of France, the threatened reduction of U.S. troops in Europe, and the invasion of Czechoslovakia. Each brought the Western defense bargain into question. Each was resolved, as the "nuclear sharing" argument was resolved, by unremitting conversation among the transatlantic allies. Taken together, they illumine both the uses and abuses of consultation among sovereign nations. But before looking more closely at these tests of cohesion, let us recall some basic facts about the Western defense system.

The allies' capacity to do enough without using nuclear weapons is the key to not having to use nuclear weapons at all. Despite all the noise about nuclear strategy, therefore, most of the bargaining in NATO is about conventional forces to defend Western Europe, the Mediterranean, and the Atlantic Ocean north of the Tropic of Cancer. The perimeter of NATO defense includes the continental United States and Canada, too. But as NATO's third decade began, the focus of defense bargaining was still on Europe and the surrounding waters.

The North Atlantic Treaty is clear about the allies' mutual defense obligations. Under Article 3, "the Parties, separately and jointly, by means of continuous and effective self-help and mutual aid, will maintain and develop their individual and collective capacity to resist armed attack." Under Article 4, they "will consult together whenever, in the opinion of any of them, the territorial integrity, political independence or security of any of the Parties is threatened." Then in Article 5, the Treaty's toothiest provision,

> . . . the Parties agree that an armed attack against one or more of them . . . shall be considered an attack against them all and consequently they agree that if such an armed attack occurs, each of them, in exercise of the right of individual or collective self-defense recognized by Article 51 of the Charter of the United Nations, will assist the Party or Parties so attacked by taking forthwith, individually and in concert with the other Parties, such action as it deems necessary, including the use of armed force, to restore and maintain the security of the North Atlantic area.

There is nothing automatic or mechanical about this modern version of the Three Musketeers' "one for all and all for one." Like the United States Constitution, the Treaty does not try to legislate what will happen if; that is left to whatever political men are in charge when the questions arise. Indeed, when the Treaty was signed in April 1949, no "NATO defense system" was in being or in prospect. Peacetime alliances had not usually featured "supreme commanders" or day-to-day political boards of directors, and the North Atlantic Treaty was, as originally conceived, an orthodox peacetime military alliance. Old-timers at NATO still like to recall that the U.S. Marine Band at the Washington signing ceremony played two Gershwin numbers which described the organization's condition and foretold its future: "I Got Plenty of Nothin'" and "It Ain't Necessarily So."

The Soviets, however, were changing things in the spring of 1949. Having clamped down on their Eastern neighbors (their 1948 take-over in Czechoslovakia helped Congress decide to pass the Marshall Plan for European recovery), they tried to squeeze the Western allies out of Berlin in 1948–49, and sponsored the invasion of South Korea in 1950. By the end of that year the new North Atlantic Council had appointed everybody's favorite wartime hero, General Dwight D. Eisenhower, as Supreme Allied

Commander for Europe. Before long there were half a million American troops in or afloat around Europe. By 1954, through a series of interlocking agreements, West Germany became a more-or-less sovereign state, a more-or-less equal NATO ally, and a partner in European defense.

The planning for how the allies would fight a war together was "integrated." Thousands of officers and men wearing different national uniforms were folded into one international command structure, and their governments agreed that if aggression occurred, a "reinforced alert" would bring their national forces under international command as well. Each government, however, would have had a chance to decide in an emergency just where its interest lay and what it would actually do. If the Treaty had made the response automatic or cooperation mandatory, neither the United States Senate nor most of the other Western legislatures would ever have ratified it. Nevertheless, the complicated and well-publicized planning machinery created a presumption that whatever was done would be done, and decided, together.

To administer this presumption, the fifteen member governments maintain in continuous service fifteen Missions to NATO, headed by Ambassadors who form the North Atlantic Council between its Ministerial meetings; a Secretary General with an international staff of nearly a thousand persons; fourteen Military Representatives, typically four-star generals or admirals, who constitute the NATO Military Committee; fifteen Political Advisors, who staff the growing political consultation arm of the Council; fifteen economists who make up the Council's Committee of Economic Advisors; resident or traveling representatives to perhaps a hundred other significant NATO committees; three major NATO Commanders and a dozen subordinate and regional commanders, each with a sizable planning staff. The Foreign Ministers meet at least twice a year; the Defense Ministers, especially those engaged in nuclear planning, more often than that; Finance Ministers also sometimes attend the annual pre-Christmas conclave. Presidents and Prime Ministers drop in from time to time; all U.S. Presidents since Harry Truman, who helped launch it, have visited with the North Atlantic Council.

The purpose of all this machinery is to enable governments to decide through argument and compromise how to provide a continuously modernizing defense system at attainable cost. Beyond nuclear planning, which is a special case with special consultative machinery to match, the elements of this Western defense bargain are: decisions on a common strategy; decisions on what forces will be provided to make the strategy work; decisions on who will spend how much for what, and how much spending will be done cooperatively; decisions about how NATO forces, in the "center" and on the "flanks," will be modernized, trained, deployed, and reinforced; and decisions about what allied forces will do in an emergency.

*   *   *

During the first fifteen years of NATO, its strategy was a mesh of contradictions—a Dulles policy of instant and massive nuclear retaliation that implied a minimum need for conventional defense, a NATO declaratory policy that urged governments to raise conventional forces in Europe comparable to those fielded by the Warsaw Pact countries, and a set of actual forces too large to be a "tripwire" or "plate glass window" and not large enough to be a match for the Soviets and their European allies. Eventually new weapons and new thinking about old weapons changed the strategic picture, and the Alliance's declaratory strategy followed suit. In the early 1960s the Kennedy administration proposed a new formula, which implied the conclusion that the big missiles were unusable for political blackmail or limited warfare, and announced the need for a full spectrum of capabilities. The France of de Gaulle opposed this effort to spread throughout the Alliance the obligation to do something about aggression; but soon after France pulled out of the NATO defense system, the other fourteen members adopted the new strategy as their own, though not without much debate and some misgivings.

NATO's new (1967) strategy is usually known by its nickname, "flexible response." General Lyman L. Lemnitzer, who was SACEUR for longer than any other commander, never tired of objecting to the nickname. He thought it sounded as though there was some flexibility about *whether* NATO would respond to aggression, and preferred longer and more accurate phrases like the one adopted in the 1967 Political Guidance to the Military Authorities: ". . . to provide for the employment as appropriate of one or more of direct defense, deliberate escalation, and general nuclear response, thus confronting the enemy with a credible threat of escalation in response to any type of aggression below the level of a major nuclear attack."

The essential point of "flexible response" is that there must be assurance of *some* response to aggression, together with the prospect of escalation—to theater nuclear war if necessary—because the threat of early initiation of general nuclear war is unbelievable as a deterrent to a limited attack or an incident.

The more likely contingencies are judged to be at the lower end of the spectrum, such as deliberate local attack (on West Berlin, on northern Norway, or at the Turkish Straits, for example) or "spillover" from strife inside Eastern Europe. (East Berlin in 1953, Hungary in 1956, Czechoslovakia in 1968 all had this potential, though none of them spilled over in a military way.) The sudden massive onslaught—the phalanx of Russian tanks rolling west down the North German plain toward the Channel ports, which was the standard contingency for NATO planners for many years—is judged unlikely to occur as long as the Alliance has reasonably strong forces in being.

Surprise on a big scale is not ruled out; that would be foolish. But it is downgraded in favor of a controversial concept called "political warning." The most likely contingency is an attack, or even a miscalculation, that occurs when tension is already high; therefore the buildup of political tension should give forewarning of military action. If this warning is correctly interpreted and acted on in time, then the NATO members, sensing a crisis, would get ready to fight if required. The military, who in every nation have had experience with political bosses unwilling to act on evidence of danger, are understandably skeptical of this notion. But the alternatives to this strategy of deterrence by threat of escalation are even less attractive. A truly conventional counterforce, with a nuclear backup designed merely to deter enemy use of nuclear weapons, would require a 20 to 35 per cent increase in defense spending, mostly by the European allies. A return to a declaratory policy of nuclear bluff leaves no practical courses of action between nuclear war and strategic surrender if the bluff were called. The "new" strategy may not be the best conceivable, but it is the best attainable.

*   *   *

A strategy of flexible and managed escalation obviously requires a system of flexible and managed consultation. The multilateral bargain has therefore become more explicit and more systematic in the 1960s—less an annual act of faith, more the product of analysis, than it had been before. An initiative by Dirk Stikker while he was NATO's Secretary General, followed up strongly by Secretary McNamara and U.K. Defense Minister Denis Healey who sent some of their best people to Paris for the purpose, finally produced a planning system in which money, equipment, and manpower were all related to each other.

The forces supporting NATO strategy are now expressed in a rolling five-year defense plan, the first full version of which was adopted in January 1969 for the period from 1969 to 1973. For the first year of each quinquennium, each country makes an explicit commitment: what divisions and squadrons and naval units and combat support arrangements it will maintain, at what standards of manning and equipment, supported by what levels of national defense expenditure. This form of consultation is designed to produce, not an integrated defense system in peacetime, but lines of national military preparation so parallel in peacetime that they can be quickly integrated under NATO commands if necessary.

NATO is a defensive alliance. That means it has no plans for starting a war, or invading Eastern Europe, or changing communist minds or social systems by force. How the West fashions its defense thus depends on assumptions about whether, where, how, and with what the Soviets might attack. (Nobody thinks the smaller countries of Eastern Europe are likely to commit aggression without the Soviets, nor is there much doubt in the West that such an attack could be readily contained.)

We know, roughly, the dimensions of Soviet defense spending and the military structure (numbers of divisions, ships, tanks, planes) they spend it on. The same goes for their Warsaw Pact allies. It is inherently impossible to know what they may do collectively with the more than a million men they keep under arms in Eastern Europe and the bordering military districts of the Soviet Union. For every declaration of peace there is a Soviet-started crisis in Berlin, Cuba, or Czechoslovakia. For every assurance of harmless intentions—the Warsaw Pact's overt war games seem to assume that NATO attacked first, just as ours assume the reverse—there is a bellicose statement of intention along the lines of President Podgorny's remarks at the Twenty-third Congress of the Soviet Communist Party in 1966, which was much analyzed and quoted around NATO at the time:

> The principle of peaceful coexistence is the principle of relations among states with different social systems. It is absolutely inapplicable in the class struggle between exploiters and those exploited, in the struggle between colonialists and the oppressed peoples, in the struggle between the socialist and bourgeois ideologies. Under present conditions the implementation of this principle facilitates victories by socialism in economic competition with capitalism and favors the successful struggle of all detachments of the world workers and national liberation movements.

Intentions being indecipherable, and quickly changeable anyway, the Western force planner is thrown back on capabilities. He is constrained in his calculations by a political judgment that in the absence of an obvious crisis the taxpayers will compel a policy of "less than the Pact, but enough."

The key judgments should of course emerge from a comparison between the Warsaw Pact's military capacities and NATO's. As long as "massive retaliation" was the doctrine, it did not seem to matter so much what the Warsaw Pact had, since the Soviets were presumably deterred by bombs and missiles from Nebraska, not by bazookas and mortars from nearby. But with the flexible strategy came a new requirement for close comparison of NATO and Warsaw Pact forces in every category. It is strange but true that a professional effort to do this was started only in NATO's nineteenth year. Even then, the mathematics of equivalence has proved elusive to military expert and systems analyst alike, and has produced some furious arguments between them.

At one extreme is the viewpoint expressed by most NATO military leaders: the Warsaw Pact's conventional capability so far exceeds that of NATO that the time it would take to overrun the NATO forces in Central Europe Region is "better measured by the clock than a calendar." The other extreme, which was pushed hard by the systems analysts of the McNamara era, is that since NATO has more men under arms and spends more money on its forces than the Warsaw Pact, it should be able to hold its own without recourse to nuclear weapons.

The "truth" presumably lies somewhere in between, and varies with the scenarios and assumptions used. You can make it true that the two alliances have about the same number of men under arms (the totals are terribly sensitive to assumptions about what proportion of U.S. and Soviet forces are counted as in or out). A sizable percentage of NATO's men are Italians, Greeks, and Turks, many of them good fighting men but neither equipped nor realistically available to fight anywhere but at home. But even if you limit the equation to troops likely to be available in the "center," the manpower comparison is still not so unfavorable: NATO has two-thirds as many men, half as much equipment, perhaps a third as many tanks, and two-thirds as many strike/attack aircraft (that is, aircraft designed to attack ground targets) as the Warsaw Pact has.

In comparing ground forces, what you count depends on what you want to prove. If you are advocating bigger Western defense budgets, you compare "divisions." NATO has about 30 of every description against more than 90 (not all of which are ready either) for the Soviets and their allies in Eastern Europe. The Institute of Strategic Studies in London, which is by far the best public source for such comparisons, thinks the Soviets could attack—with advance maneuvers which would provide some advance warning—with 70 divisions against 25 for NATO. But what is this abstraction called a "division"? Timothy Stanley, who was U.S. Defense Adviser at NATO, points out that "the United States takes about 40,000 men and about half a billion dollars in investment and operating costs and calls that block of resources *one* division: the Soviets call a similar block of resources between two and three divisions. Thus translated into Soviet terms, NATO's strength is more like sixty-odd divisions."

Similarly in air power, it is not just how many aircraft each side has on hand, but how good they are, how accurate are their maintenance crews, how well trained are their pilots, how sophisticated are the air defenses they have to penetrate, what stocks of ammunition are within easy reach, what reserves and replacements are quickly available, how vulnerable are the airfields they propose to use, and above all how the commanders and pilots rate themselves and their opposition. If an F-4 Phantom is likely to shoot down three or four MiG-21s before it gets hit—or, what is less likely, vice versa—what does it mean to compare the numbers of strike/attack aircraft?

Yet sober and honest officers will tell you the Warsaw Pact has twice as many first-line planes as NATO and forget to mention that most of the discrepancy is in air defense, not in strike/attack aircraft. They will describe the Warsaw Pact "threat" to the central front as more than a million men, against perhaps three-quarters of a million for NATO, without reminding you of the War College dictum that [the attacker needs two or three times as many men as the defender. (This conventional wisdom applies to conventional war; nobody knows about nuclear war.] They will speak of NATO manpower without explaining that the Western allies have committed to NATO varying proportions of their men under arms; some of those armed but uncommitted men, ranging from one-fifth to four-fifths of national totals, would surely be available in a real pinch.

Nor can the comparison be made only with building blocks like divisions and major items of equipment. Each kind of military power has to find its place in the equation—and those which can be somehow measured and counted, like firepower and frequency and speed, are not necessarily less relevant than those which cannot, like morale and tactical doctrine and the advantages and liabilities of surprise.

After listening to this debate for four years, the layman is bound to be impressed less by the "facts" than by their paradoxical quality. [NATO does spend more on equivalent numbers of armed men; Western military leaders will not concede that we spend defense money less efficiently than do the Soviets and their friends; yet we are, they say, far behind and need to spend much more. Air Force experts will concede that NATO is outnumbered in aircraft, but many of them are convinced that NATO would win the air battle anyway. The interesting question, as Timothy Stanley says, is how the pessimists can be as right as they are about NATO's real capacity to fight while the optimists are as right as *they* are about what a good defense it should be possible to buy with the money the Western allies are spending.

*   *   *

What the Western allies buy costs more every year; nowhere in a modern economy does money lose its value faster than in paying for advanced weapons systems. The rate of innovation is extraordinarily high. It took only a decade to get from subsonic to supersonic jet fighters. A fighter plane cost $50,000 in 1944, but you need more than $2 million in 1969 to buy a complicated mass of electronics and aerodynamics to perform the comparable function today—with probably less chance of success in the dangerous environment of modern air defense technology. As complexity grows, more education and longer training is needed to secure people who can design, produce, and operate the new systems. The only thing that comes cheaper is explosive power: a single missile costing less than $1.5 million dollars, carries more power than 200,000 World War II B-17 bombers, which would have cost $37 billion. (Even so, since no one really knows the cost of nuclear "sufficiency," the spending race goes on.)

Yet despite the predictable increase in the cost of defense and the need to run faster just to stay in the same place, the Alliance as a whole could not honestly predict in the late 1960s that the share of gross national product devoted to defense would even be maintained. Bending to the winds of détente, most members were shaving their NATO contributions around the edges.

As a matter of economics, there is no nation in Western Europe that could not easily contribute more to the common defense; and the same is true of Canada and the United States. The European average before the Soviet invasion of Czechoslovakia was hardly more than 4.5 per cent of GNP, with Canada well below that. That our allies hold their contributions to this level is a political judgment, not an economic necessity.

Canada, Belgium, and Denmark, the allies with the worst record, are subject to domestic political pressures which seem largely immune to external, or even much internal, argumentation. Iceland has no armed forces at all; the United States staffs the so-called Iceland Defense Force under a bilateral but NATO-related agreement. Luxembourg's contribution is also tiny. Portugal spends a bigger part of its GNP on defense than any other ally except the United States, but it is spent containing the Africans in Angola and Mozambique, not contributing to the common de-defense of the NATO area. France is a special case, discussed in Chapter 6. In Italy the inhibition against demobilizing soldiers and thus increasing unemployment keeps the spending up but the cost-effectiveness down. West Germany might be brought to do more; but an increased effort which would make it even more obviously the strongest military power in Western Europe conjures up political ghosts among its neighbors both East and West. Britain is reducing its over-all defense expenditures as part of a general austerity program; but as forces are brought back from East of Suez, some of them are being contributed to NATO. The Netherlands, which alone contributed as much after Czechoslovakia as we did, has had a good record but faces growing domestic political constraints.

At the same time, as Secretary General Brosio pointed out whenever he could, military spending in the Soviet Union and Eastern Europe has increased at a rate at least equivalent to the growth of their economies, which has itself been, in most cases, faster than in the NATO countries. The Soviet Union's GNP, slightly lower per capita than that of most European countries, Eastern or Western, is only some 40 per cent of the United States economy. Yet the share of its GNP devoted to defense is much the same as ours and about twice what its allies, or ours, feel able to spend. (In terms of maintaining world peace and fostering domestic tranquillity, it would of course be nice if we could get Soviet and U.S. spending down to the European average.)

One way to save money is to spend it together instead of separately. For nearly two decades in NATO, the allies have pooled more than a $100 million annually to build airfields, lay pipe, string wire, erect headquarters buildings and even, latterly, buy a space satellite for communications. Yet this "infrastructure" program is hard to expand, because the military services of each nation prefer to spend their own money on their own national products, even if it is wasteful of scarce resources to handle construction that way.

Take our own case. When NATO started, we put up most of the money for "infrastructure" while other forces used most of the facilities. But in recent years we have reversed the cost-benefit ratio; that is, our share of the cost is now less than our "usership" of the facilities bought with the pooled funds. We therefore have a clear interest in a larger program in which the Europeans help pay for facilities which the United States would otherwise have to fund by itself.

Strangely enough, the budget folk who ask for the money and the Congressmen who grant it have been slow to see this opportunity and are more inclined to try to shave the percentage of the pool we contribute—about one-quarter of the total. This is of course the traditional reaction of Congress in making contributions to international organizations; but in this case a vigorous effort to change the burden-sharing formula even more in our own favor would probably result in European decisions to do less, not more, through the pooled fund, thus leaving the funding of additional facilities for American forces entirely to the United States. We could raise the American flag over the resulting facilities; but the American taxpayer would be paying through the nose for the privilege.

When it comes to buying equipment, nationalism is equally in evidence. If our European allies bought their ships and shoes and sealing wax from the most efficient producers in Europe, instead of following their national flags with their Defense Ministry checkbooks, the savings would be enormous. Altogether, NATO Europe plans to spend some $90 billion on defense during the five years from 1969 through 1973, according to the plans each nation has submitted. Of this, our European allies will spend on the order of $25 billion on routine procurement, which leaves out the glamorous and sophisticated items such as combat aircraft. "The application of 'learning curves' and British and American experience with centralizing supply management so as to increase purchasing power, promote standardization, reduce inventory and lower warehousing costs, suggest that savings of 15 to 25 per cent should be attainable by pooling even half of this amount." Such prospective savings are certainly not to be disdained; a saving of around $5 billion would look big even in the U.S. federal budget.

The most conspicuous failure of the NATO allies to consult or cooperate in defense matters has been in the production of major items of military equipment. This part of the Western defense bargain was neither struck nor even seriously negotiated in the 1960s. A common Atlantic market in military procurement is potentially one of the most promising, yet actually the most divisive, topic of transatlantic conversation.

In practice each major ally has tended to concentrate on trying to sell the end-products of its own industry; American efforts along this line have produced a backlash, pushing the Europeans more and more towards efforts, however uneconomic, to produce tanks and planes that are conceived and produced in Europe. The decision to develop and produce major combat aircraft for the Alliance, for example, is so excruciating a process that for eight years this naturally international task has been undertaken as a strictly national one. When Robert McNamara was Secretary of Defense, he used to say that cooperative defense production requires "too much executive time and trouble." As a consequence the only "new start" in this field since the days of the Eisenhower administration (which was the era of plenty in U.S. aid funds available to lubricate international cooperation) has been the Communications Satellite program on which the main initiative had to come from the U.S. Mission to NATO.

Through NATO projects, Europe can acquire modern weapons systems (and of course civil systems for peaceful uses too) in a way which accommodates their economic needs but which also helps the U.S. balance of payments through license fees and direct purchase of equipment in the United States. There are opportunities, like the next generation of air defense systems, for associating some European research and development funds with our own, and thus perhaps lead to substantial transatlantic cooperation projects later on. Our own budgetary squeeze may make this a more attractive prospect in the 1970s than it was regarded by the Defense Department in the 1960s.

One example will suffice. During the early and mid-1970s, the tactical aircraft fleets of many NATO countries will have to be replaced. To fill this need, Europeans (mainly the British and the Germans) have designed the so-called MRCA-75 multi-role combat aircraft; its development has featured a monumental tug-of-war between the British and the Germans, but at this writing they are still pulling on the same piece of rope. That the United States is not a part of this project is directly the fault of U.S. policy which tried, long after it was futile, to sell finished made-in-America end-products to European governments which wanted to help design and make what they use, and really meant it. The U.S. Defense Department justified its disinterest in multilateral projects by citing the advantages of bilateral sales to the U.S. balance of payments. But when the American salesmen failed in competition after competition, it began to occur to the political leadership that a selling program that doesn't sell doesn't earn any money.

It is certainly not in our interest to foster European autarchy in what should be an Atlantic common market for defense-buying. But serving our interests, which happen to run with NATO's, will require a new attitude toward multilateralism. We will, for example, have to change some sacred-cow procurement policies. It is broadly accepted doctrine in the U.S. military services that nothing should be bought that cannot be used anywhere in the world. Yet if we are going to work with our European allies in designing a plane or a tank which is appropriate to the European environment, they are not going to want to pay for all the other characteristics that would make it useful in the jungles of Vietnam as well. Therefore we are going to have to be willing to buy for our own use in Europe some of the tanks and planes produced by Atlantic cooperation. That will involve setting aside our traditional "general-purpose-worldwide" preference. If the national interest is demonstrably served, it may even be possible to change an Air Force procurement policy.

*　　　*　　　*

In that arithmetic swamp called NATO force planning, where the giants of systems analysis and military expertise clash by night, how does the poor decision-maker make a good decision? "Less than the Pact, but enough" is not as clear an objective as, say, the moon. Nevertheless, the Soviets have been deterred, thus some of the force-planning decisions may have been about right. Amidst the slings and arrows of outraged analysts, the 1969 consensus in NATO was clear: its present forces are quantitatively enough but need some real improvements in quality. These improvements would not be expensive: 4 per cent more than present plans, plus better use of what is already being spent, would do the trick. It is not enough to throw a would-be aggressor back on his heels. But if the strategic aim is to make any conflict fierce enough for escalation to be probable, the aggressor would be denied an easy *fait accompli* and therefore be deterred from starting at all.

What kinds of quality improvements? The complex consultations that are summarized in NATO's five-year force plan leave no doubt on this score: any marginal savings or spending increases should be concentrated on readiness and mobility, rapid reinforcement and quick mobilization plans, and on shoring up the defense of the "flanks," especially in the Mediterranean.

The key to the defense of Central Europe is "ready" air and ground forces, plus the capacity to augment their ability to fight as tension rises. For example:

● NATO already has a good supply of aircraft to help in defense if the nations that own them can resist the temptation to reserve most of them for the nuclear war now regarded as the least likely contingency in Europe.

● It is important to make sure these planes are not caught on the ground (the way the Egyptian air force was in the Six-Day War of June 1967) by building more and better aircraft shelters, preparing quick dispersal plans, and buying the kinds of planes that can take off vertically or from very short runways.

• Our air defense is usable against aircraft coming in at high altitudes. The Soviets know this and are developing (as we are) the ability to come in low. Finding and funding the technical response to this challenge is very tough and very urgent.

• Soviet emphasis on tanks, an old Russian prejudice, does not require that NATO match Soviet numbers. But it does suggest a lot more emphasis on projectiles that do not bounce off heavy armor.

• The conventional defense of Western Europe depends critically on getting supplies and reinforcements from North America, and despite what the military air people now promise to do in the 1970s, the heavy stuff has to come mostly by sea. The Soviets know this and have invested heavily in a submarine fleet that is now the world's largest. If you ask a front-line general in Europe what would be his highest priority, he might surprise you by saying "anti-submarine warfare."

• The jumbo jets of the 1970s will be able to bring whole divisions from America to Europe, or transport units with their heavy equipment from place to place along the long NATO defense line. But we are farther along in building the big planes than in arranging for their reception. And there is no reason why the fields and roads and warehouse systems need to be built by Americans just because the planes are American.

• NATO's forward ground forces are mostly cumbersome and slow in getting to where the action is. U.S. experience with air mobility— including the massive use of helicopters both for ferrying troops and as third-dimension artillery—may be useful. Helicopters cost money, however, and the U.S. Army and Air Force are far from convinced that the experience gained in Vietnam is transferable to Europe.

Over time, if improvements like these cannot be financed and NATO's forces continue to decline in the face of rising costs, it will be necessary to consider a radical shift in how the troops that can be paid for should be put together as a defense force. Present deployments are more the product of history than of reason. The U.S. Seventh Army is in southern Germany not because that is the most vulnerable front but because that was the American sector of occupied Germany agreed to at Yalta a generation ago—and it has always seemed too expensive to move. If NATO strategists were to start from scratch, they would probably devise a specialized "forward defense" element, backed up by mobile defense using fewer but better armored formations to counterattack any penetrations. U.S. forces, also fewer but better, could then serve as a tactical reserve for SACEUR instead of being tied down to the defense of one part—and not the most dangerous part—of the front. This is a suggestion, not a forecast; the military objections and the political controversy would provide a high noise-level around NATO for a year or two before so radical a restructuring were to be adopted.

*   *   *

Mobility and quick reaction are also the dominant leitmotiv in the defense of "the flanks"—NATO's euphemism for Norway's sparsely populated north and for a weak Greece and an exposed Turkey in the south. Only beyond Norway's northernmost provinces and the mountains of eastern Turkey does the NATO defense system share a frontier with the Soviet Union—unless you count the U.S.-Soviet near-frontier in the Bering Straits. Local forces are obviously inadequate; defense of the "flanks" means getting ready mobile forces to faraway places in a hurry to help the local defenders in time.

Personally, I would prefer to suppress the word "flank" altogether. It is all right for explaining antique battles to schoolchildren; the Charge of the Light Brigade would have gone better if the commanders had worried more about their flanks. But the NATO defense system is or ought to be a whole, designed to react to a threat in any part of the treaty area. From the vantage point of Norwegians, Greeks, and Turks, their territory is not a flank but the center. From our vantage point as the main sources of mobile reinforcements, the center of the NATO defense system at any given time is wherever the threat threatens.

The first line of defense is of course the local forces; "self help and mutual aid" is still the watchword, and the troops already on the spot have to be good enough to persuade a well-equipped neighbor that he cannot bring off a costless *coup de main*. The first line of allied reinforcement is the ACE (Allied Command Europe) Mobile Force, which could send air squadrons and ground battalions of several nationalities, under NATO command, either north or south in a matter of days. Behind the mobile force are small slices of naval power, under NATO command in peacetime, to show the multiple flags of the Alliance and deter by the promise of more to come: the Standing Naval Force, a small year-round continuous maneuver in the Atlantic, and the Naval On-Call Force in the Mediterranean. Behind these flag-showing exercises are the navies of the Alliance, including the U.S. Sixth Fleet in the Mediterranean with its air power convertible to conventional or nuclear missions and its own Marines. And behind the navies is the Quick Reaction Air Force —some 300 ready U.S. aircraft—and the U.S. strategic reserve, whatever part of it is not occupied elsewhere at the time.

Greece and Turkey, which need the most help, erect the highest political hurdles. They have received more military aid, and exhibit a livelier desire to reserve it for warring on each other, than any of our other allies. Three times in the 1960s they almost fell to fighting over Cyprus. Each time they were restrained partly by the personal intervention of the President of the United States; the last time, in 1967, President Johnson's emissary Cyrus Vance was reinforced by the bold if private diplomacy of Manlio Brosio, shuttling back and forth between Athens and Ankara with a mediation mandate from the North Atlantic Council. When Greece and Turkey are not competing for Cyprus or for foreign aid, they are arguing about imaginary dotted lines of naval command in the Mediterranean Sea. And at times their way of conducting their own political life creates embarrassments for other allied governments, whose domestic constituencies remember the Treaty's words about safeguarding "the freedom, common heritage and civilization of their peoples, founded on the principles of democracy, individual liberty and the rule of law," and to "contribute toward the further development of peaceful and friendly international relations by strengthening their free institutions. . . ."

For allies to complain about each other's internal affairs has traditionally been taboo; if Belgian linguistic rivalries, U.S. race policy, German coalition politics, and the like were fair game in the North Atlantic Council, there would be no end to the trouble —and there would probably be an end to the Alliance. In private, of course, national representatives discuss their political troubles at home, frequently and with anguish; sometimes it seems that the main task of a NATO diplomat is to explain *in camera* to his colleagues the internal political factors that justify behavior by his government that would be otherwise inexplicable.

The repressive regime of the Greek colonels has created special pressures. The Danish government regularly finds some way to make clear in NATO its distaste for the Greek officers who keep in exile their attractive young King and his Danish queen. Although the damage to democracy in Greece is understandably hard for democratic politicians to take without protest, there is a strong consensus in NATO that the North Atlantic Council is not the place to press the protest. The idea that NATO should "do something" to keep its members' internal behavior up to some standard set by the Alliance is too close for Western comfort to the Brezhnev Doctrine and the invasion of Czechoslovakia by allies. Every political leader in the West understands the danger, though some of them conveniently forget it when popular and parliamentary pressures at home need to be relieved by a gesture abroad.

Beyond defense of NATO territory, there is the self-imposed obligation to defend the members' forces in the Mediterranean Sea. It is here that the balance of power has shifted the most in the 1960s. The U.S.S.R. has parlayed the turbulence at the eastern end of the sea (which of course it helped foment) into a major effort to become, for the first time in its history, a Mediterranean power.

Until 1963 Soviet submarines and other warships were infrequently sighted in the Mediterranean; by 1966 the Soviet fleet there increased tenfold. The Red Navy had learned to support itself for long periods at sea and was using Egyptian and Syrian ports for prolonged "goodwill visits" during which the visiting vessel lay in drydock nursed by Soviet technicians. During and just after the Six-Day War some 46 Soviet ships were operating in the Mediterranean, including some of the latest guided-missile cruisers and about ten submarines, together with numerous support ships. Thereafter the numbers fluctuated between 30 and 50, exceeding that mark in the maneuver with which the Soviet Navy marked the twentieth anniversary of NATO in 1969. Some of the Soviet naval missiles can reach beyond the range of any naval gun, whereas U.S. doctrine has stressed carrier air power and neglected the ship-based long-range missile. The 1968 appearance of the *Moskva*, one of two helicopter carriers built in the Black Sea, added yet another dimension to the Soviet presence. And to overcome the shortage of carrier aircraft for reconnaissance, the Soviets started doing their surveillance from bases in Egypt, using planes with Egyptian markings.

The public rationale for all this new investment leaned heavily on the claim that, as *Izvestiia* declared in November 1968, the Soviet Union is a "Black Sea power and as such a Mediterranean power too. Therefore it is directly concerned with the peace and security of this area located in the direct vicinity of the southern Soviet borders." The Mediterranean should become a "sea of peace," an aim readily accomplished if the United States would remove *its* presence from the area. A few months later the Soviet Navy conducted a joint maneuver with some Bulgarian ships in the Mediterranean, presumably to underline again the special rights of Black Sea powers, and perhaps to add a little Warsaw coloration to its southern confrontation with NATO.

The Kremlin's true purpose is not obscure. The Soviets cannot hope to match the U.S. Sixth Fleet in general-war potential; if the balloon went up, their "presence" would soon be blown out of the water—though not in the 24 hours predicted by Denis Healey in a momentary fit of hyperbole. If, however, one assumes not general war but general peace, with plenty of opportunities for gunboat diplomacy around the Mediterranean littoral, then the Soviet strategy is eminently sensible. They may indeed have found persuasive our own Navy's emphasis on the military flexibility and political utility of maritime power in peacetime.

NATO has not found in this Soviet example of "flexible response" a reason to increase the already large navies in the Mediterranean, though the British found in it a reason to hold for use there some of the maritime forces they decided in 1967 to pull back from East of Suez. But the Soviets' short-of-war flexibility was in itself alarming to an Alliance which was well organized to conduct a general war in the Mediterranean but not organized at all to operate internationally short of "Reinforced Alert." From the U.S. perspective this was an especially wide gap in the President's options: if maritime forces were needed in the Mediterranean area for political or limited military purposes, he had only two choices: use the Sixth Fleet unilaterally, or do nothing—and this in a period of Vietnam-induced backlash at home against the unilateral employment of American forces overseas.

To close the gap the U.S. Mission to NATO suggested during 1967 that NATO agree to internationalize two tasks: watching the Soviet naval squadron from the air, and matching its potential as a short-of-war flotilla. The proposals traveled a rocky road and were almost buried in a watery grave: the U.S. Navy, some of whose officers had thought up the new ideas in the first place, was hoping to use the Soviet Mediterranean presence to justify more ships and was reluctant to settle instead for giving up ships and planes to international use, even if they remained under the over-all control of American admirals wearing NATO hats. "Procedures," said one salt, "are no substitute for forces."

The military barriers yielded to political argumentation in time. During 1968 a commander of NATO maritime air surveillance was appointed by SACEUR (the appointee just happened to be also the American commander of the comparable U.S. function in the area), and in 1969 a Naval On-Call Force in the Mediterranean was established by NATO's Defense Planning Committee. The "on-call" idea was suggested by Vice Admiral John Lee of MLF fame, as an imaginative fallback from the notion of reproducing in the Mediterranean the Standing Naval Force already in operation in the Atlantic. It is a flexible formula whereby SACEUR, through his Southern Command, can call up whatever collection of maritime power is required to prepare for regional trouble or to counter Soviet moves in the Mediterranean; in the absence of trouble, he will periodically exercise, for practice, various sizes and shapes of international naval force.

We could tell by an infallible sign when the Navy decided that more good than harm might come from placing part of American power in the Mediterranean under NATO command: the projects we civilians had been pushing acquired official Navy-issue nicknames. The North Atlantic Alliance now parades in the Mediterranean as COMMARAIRMED and COMNAVOCFORMED.

*   *   *

Beyond the eternal triangle of men, materials and money, the strategy of flexible and politically managed response also requires an effectively international facility for military command and control, topped off with a system for crisis consultation among governments. These in turn require a dependable communications net, agreed procedures for crisis diplomacy, and trained participants in capitals and at NATO headquarters, working together frequently in real or hypothetical emergencies. The great recent improvements among these lines are quite directly the result of NATO's strategic shift from "massive retaliation" to "flexible response" in the 1960s.

When NATO's political headquarters moved from Paris to Brussels in October 1967, the Council decided to build into the new building a modern Situation Center, complete with up-to-date visual aids and serviced by a new NATO-wide communication system, which can flash good news or bad to fifteen capitals simultaneously in minutes. At moments of crisis the Council's Committee of Political Advisers, in earlier times a once-a-week mutual information society, was converted to an everyday "watch committee" producing overnight political assessments to guide NATO's military commanders. These facilities proved their value when the allies turned, the day after the invasion of Czechoslovakia, to consulting about what had happened and what it meant for Western security.

The most far-reaching break-through is scheduled for 1970, when the United States will launch a full-time NATO communication satellite. After initial reluctance to proliferate separate satellite systems, the idea of a NATO satellite found favor in Washington as the best way to build an electronic "bridge" over the physical communications gap that General de Gaulle threatened to create by withdrawing France from that NATO defense system.

Long before the launching, even before the satellite and its ground stations were manufactured, this project provided a psychological boost to an Alliance that was wondering about its future after the French withdrawal.

Even in prospect, the notion of a synchronous satellite stationed over the South Atlantic, in a position from which it can electronically "see" the whole Alliance from Turkey to Canada, symbolized the unity that the Fourteen were rediscovering. And since the satellite could hardly be launched until after NATO's twentieth anniversary, the contract to have it built was itself a wager on a need for the Alliance in the 1970s.

Chapter VI

Tests of Cohesion

"Crisis management" in an alliance is usually taken to mean the ways in which the partners will work together to deter or oppose an armed attack. But in peacetime the allies' relations with each other, the arguments about who will do what when with whom, provoke the crises that require the most managing.

Some of these are so deep and so slow in developing that they resemble not so much a sudden seizure as a chronic psychosis requiring fundamental analysis and prolonged therapy. Such a malady was the craving for instant peace that came over the governments of the West in the mid-1960s. The story of its diagnosis and of the medicine the allies prescribed for themselves is told in Chapter 7.

Of the three more dramatic crises of the late 1960s, two—General de Gaulle's pullout and efforts by some Americans to follow his example partway—came from unilateral efforts to change the rules of the transatlantic bargain. A third spasm was the agony of reappraisal after the invasion of Czechoslovakia in 1968. Each tested the sticking quality of the glue that holds the Western Alliance together. From each, to the astonishment of its premature mourners, the Alliance emerged with adaptations that made its members better able to cope with the next crisis.

*　　　*　　　*

There was plenty of political warning for the French attack on the transatlantic bargain. Talking to President Kennedy in 1961 —it was the only time they met—de Gaulle drew a sharp distinction between the Alliance itself, as defined in the Treaty, and NATO as the organization which grew out of it. He urged reorganizing NATO. Arthur Schlesinger reports his reasoning: Since the European countries could no longer be confident that the United States would use nuclear weapons first, they themselves had to assure their future security, not without but also not exclusively through the United States. No U.S. President could reject out of hand the notion that the Europeans should take care of more of their own defense, and Kennedy tried hard to find out just what kind of change in NATO the General had in mind. He elicited only "vague generalities" in reply. As Kennedy later on summed up his mystification, "A coherent policy cannot call for both our military presence and our diplomatic absence."

The Nassau deal of December 1962, which gave Britain access to American nuclear systems that were not available to France, did nothing to disabuse de Gaulle of the notion, formed long before in dealing with Roosevelt and Churchill, that "les Anglo-Saxons" would never dependably cooperate with France—which, in his talking and writing, he tends to identify both with Europe and with himself. By 1965 de Gaulle was announcing the end of military integration at least by NATO's twentieth birthday, four years later. In February 1966, after his re-election to a seven-year term as President, he announced at a press conference that France would withdraw forthwith from NATO. The French Foreign Office, trying to understand what the policy was supposed to be, prepared elaborate plans for a gradual withdrawal and polite notes to allies suggesting that NATO installations and headquarters then on French soil might be more welcome elsewhere in Europe. The papers were sent out to the President's country place in the village of Colombey-les-deux-Eglises for review over a weekend. Instead of agreeing, de Gaulle wrote letters in his own handwriting to President Johnson and the heads of the British, German and Italian governments, relegating the smaller states to typewritten notes from the Foreign Office. I mean it, the General thundered. NATO and all its military works will get out of France, and France will escape "subordination" by getting out of NATO.

Despite the political warning, or perhaps because de Gaulle had said it so often without doing it, the French action was an enormous shock in every allied capital. It shattered a basketful of gentlemen's agreements with a notable absence of gentleman-liness. It denounced five U.S.-French bilateral agreements about logistic and communications arrangements on French territory, even though four of these agreements explicitly provided for denunciation only by mutual agreement. It required the exodus within a year of the NATO, American, and Canadian military headquarters for Europe as well as the office of the Central Region commander, (a French general) and the head offices of a number of technical bodies. And it pulled all French officers and enlisted men out of NATO's integrated planning staffs.

In order to justify his action, de Gaulle had to pretend that he did not understand NATO "integration," that he thought combined planning made it automatic to cooperate in combined operations in a defense emergency. He certainly knew better. He was actually denouncing, not the Treaty or even the joint planning, but the presumption of cooperation in unknown future contingencies. He hoped to be able to be at his allies' side if they were attacked, he told visitors during this period; but that decision could only be made by France (read President de Gaulle) at the time.

There was, of course, nothing illegal about thus denying a presumption. No NATO country is or can be bound by its Treaty obligations to take specific, concrete acts. Why, then, this elaborate scenario to escape an automaticity that everybody in the know knew did not exist?

The mystery of motivation deepened as it became clear how very selective General de Gaulle's "withdrawl from NATO" was to be:

● He did not pull the two French divisions out of Germany. Instead he made a special agreement with Bonn to keep them there, for unstated reasons which could only be to oppose an invasion of the Federal Republic. He even authorized joint planning (called "liaison arrangements") between the French commander in Germany, General Jacques Massu of Algerian fame, and NATO's local commanders; this process of course revived to some extent the presumption of cooperation which de Gaulle had so indignantly denounced and so publicly destroyed.

● He did not withdraw from a long list of NATO military activities which were especially important to the defense of France, notably the air defense system, the communications net, and research and development work on the frontiers of military technology. To make sure France did not miss anything it might find useful, a high-ranking liaison office was maintained with NATO's Military Committee.

● He did not deny to the allies the use of French territory for overland communications, for the pipeline shipment of oil for U.S. and other NATO-committed forces in Germany, or even for bombing practice by the U.S. Air Force. The only provision was that no U.S. troops remain permanently on station in France.

● He was careful not to interfere in any way with use by his allies of French air space, potentially the most damaging military obstacle he could have placed in NATO's way. He did rule that authorizations would be given, not from one year to the next but only from month to month; but since all the same categories and nationalities of aircraft were permitted to fly over France that had been doing so before, this piece of shadow-boxing merely increased the paperwork in the Paris bureaucracy without adverse effect on NATO-related air operations.

The North Atlantic Council's Paris headquarters, at the Porte Dauphine overlooking the Bois de Boulogne, was not included in the ban on installations in France. De Gaulle thereby made the point that while NATO was obsolete and unnecessary, the political consultation functions of the Alliance were still within the pale. There followed several months of argument, with the United States arguing for removal but some members (notably Canada and Denmark) fearing that de Gaulle would denounce the Treaty itself if further provoked. Eventually the Council decided that it was too risky for NATO's political board of directors to be located in a nation that would not promise to leave Alliance communications intact in the event of war. The French themselves preferred that the Council stay in Paris, for it was no part of Gaullist strategy to prove to the world that Paris was no longer the center of things. But the Quai d'Orsay was tactically astute; not wishing to be on the losing side of an issue so loaded with "face," Foreign Minister Maurice Couve de Murville left the decision up to the allies. He even agreed to pay France's share of the moving costs when, after the welcoming Belgians had erected a serviceable building in a matter of months, the Council moved bag and baggage to Brussels in October 1967.

In retrospect the significant thing about the withdrawal of France from the NATO defense system is that it was not very significant. It did not destroy the Alliance—if that was the idea. It did not set France up as the Western European partner best suited to make peace with the Russians—if that was the idea. It did not remove France from dependence on the U.S. nuclear umbrella—if that was the idea. It did not even keep de Gaulle in office. The net effects were to accelerate the reduction of French influence in Europe, in favor of the Germans, and to prod the other Western allies into changing their strategy and improving their cohesion. These can hardly have been the results consciously desired by a Gaullist France.

Then why did he do it? It would be disrespectful to a man with qualities of greatness to assume that General de Gaulle could not reason from cause to effect. If the effect his action had on NATO was very small, the interesting question is: How much effect was the French pullout *intended* to have on the organization? The General surely did not think he was taking the keystone from the NATO defense system: he carefully avoided doing precisely those things which would have seriously weakened it. Besides, he must have been aware that France, which had succeeded in stalling the European Six, did not have the power to stall the Western Fifteen even if it tried; the big difference of course is the presence in NATO of the United States.

We have to assume, therefore, that the noneffect on NATO of France's semi-withdrawal was intentional, which suggests that the whole highly publicized affair was an elaborate charade designed for domestic political effect. The later opinion of one of NATO's wisest diplomats is pertinent and persuasive: "French 'withdrawal' was a cheap, anti-American gesture, which changed almost nothing militarily, certainly did not harm French security, yet enabled the General to crow that he had 'withdrawn from NATO'—for home consumption."

The crisis lasted about four months; the real story was not

in what the General did but in how the Fourteen reacted. In the first shock of the February bombshell, before the limited nature of de Gaulle's action was realized, each of the other allies had to decide whether to follow France's example. When the smoke cleared, the score was 14 to 1.

Western Europe still had to be defended, the Fourteen decided; if it had to be done for a time without France, that was politically tiresome but militarily tolerable although it would probably increase both the difficulty and the cost. The conclusion that the withdrawal of one is the destruction of all was, however, unacceptable.

The French announcement caused each of the other allied governments to look very hard at its own national interest in NATO's presumption of cooperation in an emergency. Some of them pondered whether they could get along without the American guarantee; others feared the rise of a nationalist Germany if the constraint of a working Alliance were removed; still others tried to imagine what sort of national defense program could possibly substitute for the $35 billion a year the allies other than France were investing in defense cooperation; still others wondered whether they would be left out of Europe's future peace arrangements if they left themselves out of current defense arrangements.

Each in its own way and for its own reason swiftly concluded that the continuation of NATO with or without France was essential to its own national interest. In ten days of day-and-night consultation, starting with a British draft, the Fourteen produced together a declaration of admirable clarity and, considering it was produced by diplomats and politicians, remarkable brevity. In six sentences totalling less than 150 words—that is fifteen words a day, quite a high production rate in the manufacture of political consensus—the Fourteen declared that NATO was as necessary as ever:

> The North Atlantic Treaty and the Organization established under it are both alike essential to the security of our countries.
> The Atlantic Alliance has ensured its efficacy as an instrument of defense and deterrence by the maintenance in peacetime of an integrated and interdependent military organization in which, as in

no previous alliance in history, the efforts and resources of each are combined for the common security of all. We are convinced that this Organization is essential and will continue. No system of bilateral arrangements can be a substitute.

The North Atlantic Treaty and the Organization are not merely instruments of the common defense. They meet a common political need and reflect the readiness and determination of the member countries of the North Atlantic Community to consult and act together wherever possible in the safeguard of their freedom and security and in the furtherance of international peace, progress and prosperity.

The group that put together this declaration of faith had no constitution, no formal structure, and no staff; to avoid arguments about leadership, the dean of NATO's Ambassadors, Belgian representative André de Staercke, chaired with energy and good cheer the group known around Paris simply as "Les Quatorze." In time, after an intricate negotiation between the American and French delegations, France agreed to stay away from meetings of the Defense Planning Committee, which, as the North Atlantic Council minus one, took final decisions on all questions affecting those parts of the NATO defense system from which France had withdrawn. De Gaulle's favorite distinction turned out to be useful: the Fourteen managed "NATO," and the Fifteen consulted together on political issues in "the Alliance."

Historians of this little drama may be puzzled by the absence of public invective by the Fourteen to match the outrageously haughty and unilateral behavior of the President of France. Maintaining a façade of almost exaggerated official politeness was not easy, but it was deliberate, and universally judged to be necessary. Private citizens, journalists, and politicians out of office were outspoken, and in the United States a flurry of boycotts temporarily slowed the importation of French wines and cheeses. But President Johnson, whose private references to General de Gaulle stretched his considerable talent for colorful language, imposed an icy correctness on those who had reason to discuss French policy in public. Some governments even turned the other cheek: Canada, with its restless French-speaking minority, insisted for months that NATO should act as though nothing had happened and postpone or avoid allied actions in which the French were not prepared to participate.

From one of my frequent commuting runs to Washington during this period, I managed to return with a lucid instruction about the general attitude the Fourteen might adopt in dealing with their reluctant semi-partner. It was a deceptively permissive policy:

- We would maintain and modernize the NATO defense system, with France if possible, without it if necessary.
- We would hope for as much cooperation as possible from France, but would refrain from arguing with the French government about the extent of that cooperation. We would simply try to establish how far the French were willing to go along with the rest of us in each sector of the defense system and adjust to that.
- At the same time we would arrange things so that no aspect of the defense of Western Europe would be critically dependent on French cooperation in an emergency. That meant building bypass communication systems, deciding on a NATO communications satellite, and working up plans for flying around instead of over France if necessary.

This line of reasoning turned out to parallel the conclusions reached in other capitals of the Alliance, and became the basis for dozens of detailed jurisdictional deals that drew a clear if wavy line between the defense of France and the defense of Europe. The illogic of some of these arrangements disturbed no one; at lunch that summer, my French colleague and I agreed that if Descartes was revolving in his grave, that was more a vexation for France than for the Fourteen. It was, strangely, the would-be partisans of France who most embarrassed the French representatives on the North Atlantic Council. Canada and Denmark especially often argued with France about the degree of their cooperation, hoping to move the French far enough to make unnecessary the taking of important NATO decisions on a fourteen-nation basis.

As the new relationship with France came into focus, something happened that nobody had predicted. Even before the formal defection, France had been the most reluctant ally on changes in strategy, standardization of equipment, joint training maneuvers, and undertakings to work together in future emergencies. With France standing aside, the renewed political interest in NATO unity had a galvanizing effect on the governments that did want to cooperate in European and Mediterranean defense. By the spring of 1967 the NATO Defense Ministers had set forth the first new agreed strategy in eleven years, and had sent the first messages from one NATO headquarters to another by satellite. And quite suddenly, the mood of the Fourteen was not to brood about the possible death of their Alliance in 1969, but to plan in earnest for the 1970s. In 1967 the first draft of a five-year plan (which took two more years to mature into a full-blown system) set forth the men, the materiel, the mobility, and the money each government (except France) expected to devote to the common defense up through 1972. And the political work on the Study of the Future Tasks of the Alliance was already reaching even farther into a still uncertain but somehow less depressing future.

It is still too early to forecast the choices which a post-de Gaulle but still Gaullist France will make. French military and civilian bureaucracies cooperate in *ad hoc* fashion with the NATO bureaucracy, and the choice of more active French participation remains wide open. Among the French military there is an almost conspiratorial willingness to act on the presumption that in an emergency France would be at the side of its allies. Even before de Gaulle contrived his own political demise, his government had walked away from General Ailleret's policy of "tous azimuts"— defense against all points of the compass—which a German writer had characterized as "more a spleen than a strategy." In an address at the Institut des Hautes Etudes de Défense Nationale in March 1968, the new French Chief of Staff, Air Force General Fourquet, embraced large chunks of "flexible response," wrote off as too risky and bad for deterrence the tactic of "awaiting the enemy on one's own territory," and advocated "profiting as much as possible from the earlier effort of the allies." It is only a short step to working out with the integrated NATO planning staffs concrete measures in which France could share.

In sum, the Fourteen can defend themselves without France because the United States is there. France cannot defend itself without the Fourteen for the same reason. The way things are as 1970 begins is far from ideal, but the Fourteen can live with it better, and longer, than France can. We can therefore avoid the temptation to fashion new bilateral ties of a kind—for example, on nuclear matters—which would shake the confidence of our other allies in the soundness of their decision to work within NATO in assuring their national defense.

France can readily resume whatever degree of cooperation, on whatever timetable, is permitted by a decent consideration for the ghost of General de Gaulle. There are empty chairs and doors ajar all over the NATO headquarters in Brussels and Casteau. No public eating of berets is required, or desirable. The allies will be delighted to find France, one day, back in the club as if nothing had happened.

*   *   *

French forces in Germany are merely useful to NATO. The presence of American forces there is a "must." Since the centerpiece of NATO's deterrent is still U.S. strategic nuclear weapons, with the threat of escalation toward their use, the trigger attached to our megaton missiles is our military presence in Europe. That presence is, indeed, so crucial that most Europeans tend to downgrade their own defense effort as marginal because it is not tied to a nuclear capability. Yet from our viewpoint, European effort is what makes the American presence possible. It is true that, for example, a Danish military effort by itself makes no military sense in the modern world. But as part of what our allies do together to persuade us to do our part, even the smallest contribution makes good political and military sense.

The U.S. Defense Department resists estimating how much of our huge military budget is spent on doing our part in NATO; you can make it look large or small according to what editorial view the statistics are intended to sustain. In NATO's early years, we had to provide the muscle, the forces, the organizing talent, and the resources to prime the pump. In recent years, as European and especially German forces were trained and deployed, the balance has become somewhat more even—whether sufficiently so is what the transatlantic argument is all about. We now provide 12 per cent of the manpower, one-quarter of the air forces, by far the strongest navy, and all the tactical nuclear weapons—in sum, perhaps half of all the Alliance's military resources. But that only accounted for about $17 billion or $18 billion out of more than $80 billion Congress provided for defense in the late 1960s; consequently the U.S. share can readily be inflated for bargaining purposes by adding in, for example, part or all of our strategic nuclear forces. We could also argue that we spend 10 per cent of our gross national product on defense, while the European average is well under 4.5 per cent; this was a double-edged argument, since the biggest single part of our spending at the time was to conduct a war in Vietnam which most of our friends in Europe thought was unnecessary and unwise.

There is always a certain amount of pressure in American politics for pulling "some" U.S. troops out of Europe. Nobody seems to want them all out, and few critics of their presence there have any better rationale for a reduced number than the U.S. administration is able to concoct for the current numbers, whatever they are from year to year. Some critics are doctrinaire (advocates of unilateral disarmament) or frivolous (legislators who complain they get too many troublesome letters from American servicemen abroad and especially from their wives). But most of those seriously concerned argue the case for withdrawal on grounds of fairness: the Europeans should pick up a larger share of the check. They could well do so, as we have seen. Occasionally, after a scare such as the invasion of Czechoslovakia, they do raise the ante; generally, they do not, and the shares remain roughly the same from year to year.

In the 1960s, given the congressional pressures at their backs, none of our three Presidents was able to make the promise to maintain the numbers of our troops in Europe for a given period ahead that might have bargained European defense spending to higher levels. In the circumstances, thoughtful Europeans are bound to take any U.S. troop reductions as a sign that we see the Soviet threat as diminishing, or that we are reverting to massive retaliation, or that we have devalued the importance of Europe.

Any of these interpretations misreads the motives even of those who are most loudly beating the drums for the United States to do less. Their motivation is simpler: they are tired of responsibility, tired of defense spending, and assume that if we do less our allies will have to do more. But that is the mirage: whatever we say, no European politician would feel he could take a more serious view of Soviet intentions and capacities than the United States does. With a U.S. reduction the European effort would also be less; the leader is followed when he walks uphill and also when he walks downhill.

Most European politicians would feel the prudent answer to a U.S. withdrawal from the defense of Europe would not be to enter the arms race with the Russians in our stead, but to seek the best deal with the Russians they could. For they know, as we do, that no attainable effort on their own is likely to deter the world's other superpower. If only one of the two superpowers is interesting itself in the future of Europe, better tune the antennae toward it and accommodate to the resulting influence from the East.

In a way the most baffling American objection to our military presence in Europe comes from those who are convinced we cannot afford it. The focus here is on balance of payments. It is true that in the mid-1960s more than $1 billion of our annual hemorrhage of gold resulted from dollar spending in Europe by U.S. public agencies, predominantly military agencies. But by 1967–68 this flow had been partly stanched by "offset" purchases of arms from the United States and partly postponed by the purchase of special Treasury bonds, which constituted promises to refrain for several years from converting into gold the extra dollars the surplus countries were earning from us. In the German case, which is by far the largest flow, the current gap had been brought down to about $200 million out of nearly $900 million we would otherwise have lost; this was done by bilateral bargaining with the tough but basically cooperative Germans. Even that small gap could not endanger our gold reserves, since the German central bankers were already (in deference to our troubles) following a policy of not converting their surplus dollars into gold.

Americans preoccupied with the balance of payments often suggest a reduction in our European spending as the cure. In practice, a big drop in U.S. military spending in Europe would result in a big drop in European purchases of military equipment in the United States, and probably also an unwillingness to cooperate with our Treasury by holding surplus dollars off the gold market. If it appeared that our government really thought the dollar so weak that it was willing to undermine the NATO defense system to save a billion dollars or less, a massive flight from the dollar would be the only prudent policy for our allies and for everybody else.

We have probably gone as far as we can go—some would say farther than we should have gone—with a procedure that involves annual arm-twisting missions from Washington to Bonn. The earlier technique, called "offset payments," helped bring down the Erhard government in 1966. Even if it be granted that Erhard was no great loss and the resulting Grand Coalition, for all its internal troubles, proved a stronger and therefore more reliable ally, the continued practice of annual bilateral negotiations has had the grotesque effect of making Germans think that payments intended to help NATO are really an aid program for Uncle Sam.

The context of the balance-of-payments problem should really be multilateral. The Federal Republic is host to the forces of five other nations besides the United States (only Britain has had negotiations parallel to ours); and we have smaller payments problems with Italy, Belgium, the Netherlands, and Canada. There is consequently a place for a multilateral payments scheme, analogous to the old European Payments Union, in which the bilateral adjustments could be pooled—and made politically more palatable—by relating them to their NATO purpose. At the November 1968 Ministerial meeting the Ministers agreed to describe the problem, but stopped short of deciding to do anything about it beyond bilateral arm-twisting from year to year. In the North Atlantic Assembly, the conference of parliamentarians which has no formal power but can have considerable public influence, Senator Charles Percy of Illinois has proposed a promising multilateral scheme; with this or something like it as the basis, it is high time we stopped complaining and started consulting in the Alliance about finding practical ways to share the balance-of-payments burden of national contributions to the common defense.

It is not at all clear that if we were starting from scratch, we would place nearly a third of a million troops in Europe and the Mediterranean area. But in politics you are never starting from scratch, you are always starting from where you are, which is usually where you would prefer not to be. The political symbolism of the American presence is such that the smallest change in numbers causes tremors quite out of proportion to their size. Nevertheless, for one reason or another about 100,000 American troops were removed from the European continent in the decade of the 1960s—with a concomitant reduction in the presence of wives, children, movies, laundries, and post exchanges.

In 1961 we had 417,000 "in or afloat in" the European theater; by 1966 these were down to 366,000, partly because the brigade sent to reinforce the Berlin garrison after Khrushchev's 1961 threats was quietly taken out again later on. In NATO's withdrawal from France in 1967, 18,000 men were sent home rather than elsewhere in Europe. From time to time, the priority of fighting a war in Vietnam claimed men, planes, and ships previously committed to NATO. And in 1968 we "redeployed and dual-based in the United States" 33,000 more; they are supposed to be gone only in body but not in spirit. The story of the last of these moves is worth a moment's pause; it is a neat example of how internal and transatlantic politics interact.

*   *   *

The year was 1967, the place was Washington. Escalation of the war in Vietnam had produced an impressive backlash in the universities, on the streets, and in the United States Senate. The balance of payments looked bad, Soviet behavior (at least in Europe) looked good, and President Johnson had begun to look vulnerable. Secretary of Defense McNamara was proposing that the United States withdraw from Europe two of its five and two-thirds divisions, and most of its combat Air Force; he needed the money for the budget, and some of the men for Vietnam. Senator

Stuart Symington was sounding the alarm about the balance of payments. And the Democratic Majority Leader, Senator Mike Mansfield, was using Defense Department statistics to press a resolution calling for a deep cut in the U.S. military presence in Europe. (The number was not specified, but that season's suggestions ranged from 50,000 to 200,000.)

Even with hindsight I find it hard to understand the head of steam this proposal appeared to have generated. In a taxi headed for the Senate Office Building one morning, I jotted down a few arguments against the troop cut; after twenty-three blocks of travel, a baker's dozen had leaped to mind:

● De Gaulle failed to dissolve the glue, why do we jump to his aid?

● If we reduce, Europeans will reduce.

● Some of our nuclear weapons will have to be withdrawn. How can that fail to degrade the deterrent?

● Europeans who want neutralism, or accommodation with Soviets rather than the West, will be helped.

● The German extremists will have a better chance. This will sour their western neighbors on the Germans, who will be by far the biggest military factor on their immediate horizon. Even de Gaulle might not relish that.

● Those in Germany who want to get back on the nationalistic road will be helped. How does that help us?

● Our withdrawal makes the Non-Proliferation Treaty a harder sale. Why should Europeans sign off nuclear weapons if we are leaving?

● The idea of *mutual* force reductions can be kissed goodbye.

● Soviet penetration of the Mediterranean has sunk in deep on the Hill. Yet if we bring back divisions and squadrons from the Center, can the Sixth Fleet be far behind?

● NATO (and Berlin) are prime symbols of what we think of our international commitments. Do we convert them into symbols of our isolation?

● The savings are illusory; in the short run at least, one-time costs of withdrawal are very high.

● Balance-of-payments gap is down to peanuts. Do we dig up the whole farm to find a bag of peanuts?

● In sum: The Russians have failed to *push* us out of Europe. Are we going to let them *pull* us out by aiding Hanoi and keeping us immured in Vietnam?

These arguments did not convert those Senators bent on a heavy troop cut. Despite the powerful support for their position, however, President Johnson was unconvinced. Some of his advisers were alarmed that the Mansfield Resolution might pass the Senate; but others said a two-division withdrawal would irreversibly "unravel NATO." He asked John J. McCloy, symbol of the Establishment and expert on Germany, to be a White House consultant and suggest a policy.

McCloy possessed none of the orthodox attributes of bureaucratic power. He was not head of a great Cabinet Department; he represented no active outside pressure group; he had only a tiny staff borrowed from State and from the Pentagon's Joint Staff. But as one of the architects of NATO he could get a hearing. He could always quit in a huff that would be embarrassing to the administration if he thought the policy outcome too misguided. And he had the President's confidence, which usually counts more points than anything else in a Washington hassle.

After deep study and considerable travel, McCloy concluded that U.S. troops committed to NATO should not be reduced at all. Even before presenting this conclusion in Washington, he had helped persuade the British to delay a planned reduction of their own, and the Germans to limit a decision to slice their defense expenditures. Back in Washington, he bought with great reluctance a compromise with McNamara by which two brigades, or about two-thirds, of the Twenty-fourth Division would be brought home and "dual-based" in Kansas—still as part of the European command, still committed to NATO as first-line troops, and exercised in Germany at least once a year (to show the Europeans they had not been demobilized or sent to the Far East). A similar arrangement was applied to four of the nine U.S. combat air squadrons in Central Europe; they were eventually "dual-based" just around the corner in Mountain Home, Idaho.

The President and his Cabinet reached agreement with McCloy, and held a meeting with congressional leaders. My consultant tells me that a deeper cut would unravel NATO, he said in effect. Does any one here want to unravel NATO? Only Senator Mansfield still did.

Consulting with our Allies about the dual-basing concept was not easy either. It was important to take the initiative: we would in any event have been "hauled into court" if we had started to

move troops out without consultation, and the resulting controversy would have had some of the political effects we were trying
to avoid by not making the two-division cut. The consultation
ran through the summer and fall of 1967; we did not press for
formal action until the December meeting of NATO Defense
Ministers, and by the time that came around even the skeptics
were used to the dual-basing idea. By deciding to handle the
matter with some grace and style, and not railroad it through in
a hurry, we demonstrated that 33,000 troops could be moved
west across the Atlantic without adverse effects on the troop
levels of our European allies.

The line on further troop cuts was then clearly and publicly
drawn. On February 19, 1968, when Secretary General Brosio on
a trip to Washington met with the President, they jointly declared
that "They considered the maintenance of NATO's strength,
including the U.S. commitment, as necessary to continuing stability and security in the North Atlantic area. This stability and
security provide the basis for exploring with the U.S.S.R. the
possibility of mutual force reductions."

The Mansfield Resolution was battered but still afloat. Its
sponsor mentioned it from time to time, and claimed more than
a third of the Senate as co-sponsors. In one round of interviews
early in the 1968 session, I found no co-sponsor who could tell
me its parliamentary status; "Ask Mike," they would say. No one
in the House of Representatives seemed to think there was solid
political nourishment in pressing a European troop cut. When
the Resolution reached the Senate floor, Senators Henry D. Jack-
son and Thomas Kuchel easily disposed of it by procedural
objection: it had not gone through any substantive hearings, but
had reached the floor from the Senate's Democratic Policy Committee, an unorthodox channel for a matter of some interest both
to Armed Services and Foreign Relations. When last seen it was
languishing in a select committee in which the votes were about
evenly divided between pros and cons.

When a Majority Leader of the United States Senate fails to
bring his favorite resolution to a vote (or brings it up in a way
that is wide open to procedural objection), the outsider is entitled
to assume that the sponsor does not want to test its strength

because he does not have the votes. In any case the Resolution, like a strategic nuclear weapon, was clearly more useful when rattled than when exploded—especially since the fallout might well damage the security of the United States.

The Senator from Montana visited the communist world, including Prague, in the summer of 1968, returning convinced that the prospects for détente justified a big troop reduction in Europe. He sent the President a report to this effect, which reached the White House a few hours before the Soviet tanks rolled across the Czechoslovak frontier. In a gesture of almost superhuman political courtesy President Johnson suppressed this untimely forecast. The troop-cut proposal was dead anyway for that session. Its revival would be the next President's problem.

*　　　*　　　*

The forces of the Warsaw Pact began rolling and flying into Czechoslovakia at 11:00 P.M., European time, the evening of August 20, 1968. Ninety to one hundred and fifty minutes later, Soviet diplomats in various capitals hastened to deliver assurances that the tanks and planes were in Prague by invitation, and were not directed against the "state interests" of the United States or its allies. At 2:00 A.M., August 21, Prague radio aired news of the invasion; at 2:09 A.M. the Associated Press man in Prague, who had been having a reflective nightcap with his *New York Times* colleague when he heard the Czech broadcast, got out the first wire-service "flash." A reporter for DNA, the West German news agency, had the news earlier, from people who saw Russians taking over Prague's airport. But his desk editor back home, who had released an earlier false alarm, was so skeptical of the story that DNA missed the beat.

Picking up the AP story, Armed Forces Radio in Frankfurt broke into its all-night music with a bulletin. The SHAPE duty officer, who was listening to the jazz, heard the bulletin, alerted NATO's Brussels Situation Center, which phoned the national delegations. Meanwhile some of NATO's air defense radars were partially jammed, a by-product of Soviet jamming in Czechoslovakia, as it turned out; those responsible for round-the-clock air defense correctly diagnosed the jamming as not directed at NATO, but mistakenly discounted the jamming so heavily that this interesting bit of information never got to the political levels of the Alliance that night. Nevertheless by breakfast time in Europe, NATO's "crisis consultation" machinery was in high gear.

In later post-mortems on the sequence of events that evening, the Alliance relearned a basic lesson: the real trouble in crisis consultation is usually not an absence of fancy alert procedures or instantaneous communication systems, but the tendency of governments which get crisis information to hatch it themselves for a while before telling their allies. The Soviet Ambassadors to Western capitals were apparently instructed to ask for appointments as soon as the operation was under way, and convey messages of explanation and reassurance; many of them did not get around to doing so until the following morning, but in the major capitals they made special efforts to act immediately. The first message was delivered in Paris, an hour and a half after H-hour; Minister of State Fred Mulley was handed the British edition less than an hour later in London. Ambassador Dobrynin insisted on seeing President Johnson personally; he did so at 8:30 (Washington time) the evening of August 20, two hours and a half after the Soviet tanks started toward Prague. Thereupon time was taken in Washington for a meeting of the National Security Council and a further meeting between Dobrynin and the Secretary of State before the information was imparted to Washington's mission to NATO; and when the Dobrynin text was received in Brussels, it was unaccompanied by instructions to tell any ally about it.

In this manner Washington not only kept in the dark those allies not briefed by the Russians, but also deprived itself of the relevant information that other capitals were receiving similar Soviet messages with intriguing and significant differences. From Brussels, we burned the telephone wires to get authority to exchange information with our allies. Minutes before the North Atlantic Council met—at 10:15 A.M. August 21, eleven hours after the invasion began—the U.S. government decided to tell its allies what it knew, and I was so instructed by telephone. The British delegate similarly got last-minute instructions to tell what London knew only if the Americans did; and the French delegation could not even get that much discretion from Paris. A telegram authorizing me to do what I had already done in the morning Council session finally arrived after lunchtime.

The first big debate inside NATO was not on long-term policy but on a disturbing tactical question: Why didn't we know the invaders were going to move before they moved?

"Flexible response" rests heavily on the assumption of timely warning of any move by the Soviet Union and its allies against NATO. We would have political warning, the doctrine says, because a surprise attack not preceded by a buildup of political tension seems almost inconceivable. We would have strategic warning because we would see and sense the buildup of forces the Soviets would require to undertake a serious military operation against the NATO defense system. But it has always seemed unlikely that we could tell in advance the precise moment at which an attack by those built-up forces would be launched. There should not be any such thing as political or strategic surprise, but tactical surprise is always possible.

In the first shock of seeing Russian troops just across their Bavarian border, the Germans in particular called into question this whole set of assumptions. After a good deal of debate, however, there was rather general agreement that the events of August paradoxically validated NATO's warning doctrine. We (and the Czechoslovaks) had several months of quite visible political warning: the Soviets had been visibly distressed ever since the outline of the Dubček regime's course became clear enough for them to see danger in it and had been doing their best, without success, to dissuade the Prague "liberals" from liberalizing so fast. We had a number of weeks of strategic warning as the Soviet forces got into position to threaten the Czech leaders with a military invasion.

As far as it went, therefore, our analysis in NATO was about right. The Soviets, we thought, were massing most of their strength in Eastern Europe within striking distance of the Czech border. NATO correctly guessed that these very large military movements—the largest in Europe since World War II—were not aimed against NATO; they were clearly designed either to pressure the Czechs or, if pressure failed, to be ready for invasion. What we did not know and could not predict was whether they *would* invade—until they started to move and told us they were moving. Certainly the military plan was laid long before all the palavering in Warsaw, Cierna, and Bratislava, but the political decision was evidently taken quite late in the game.

The one addition to our prior analysis was more emphasis on the Soviet tendency to use exercises as cover for invasion preparations. The military nightmare was expressed in a difficult question from a thoughtful officer: Suppose the Soviet and Warsaw Pact troops had done all the same things they did in July and the first three weeks of August 1968, and then instead of invading Czechoslovakia, *had turned right and kept coming?*

The Soviet military move was impressively rapid, well planned, and well executed. It was of course massively overdone to meet the remote contingency of armed resistance: more than one-third of a million men, more than twenty-five ground divisions, some airlifted from as far away as the Baltic regions, and the occupation of all the large airfields in Czechoslovakia.

There was some argument about the net effect of all the military comings and goings in Eastern Europe. The systems analysts, who had been carrying Czech and Rumanian troops as loyal Warsaw Pact members, suddenly dropped them out of the calculation and sustained for a few days the extraordinary theory that the Soviet military advance into the heart of Central Europe should be comforting to the West. At the other extreme the Pavlovian reaction of military intelligence was to say that the invasion proved that the West could plan only on the basis of "capabilities," since intentions were so changeable. Actually the new Soviet dispositions—more troops, farther west, in a higher state of readiness than before—were likely to be quite temporary and therefore not at all a good basis for Western military planning. What was really scary was the quantum jump in uncertainty about Soviet intentions, for their efficient military operation was in the service of an almost childishly sloppy political scenario. If the Soviet leaders could misread their near neighbors, the Czechs, as badly as they did, how well, NATO defense experts asked, are they reading *us?*

The disturbing fact was that we did not really know what the Soviets had in mind. They had said all too clearly that they proposed to hang onto their empire no matter what. But how big is the empire they had chosen to "defend"? Rumania is hard-line communist on the inside; how independent an external policy could Bucharest get away with? How far beyond the Warsaw Pact did the "socialist commonwealth" extend? Was Yugoslavia subject to occupation in the defense of socialism? In whose "camp" did the Soviet leaders place Albania? Beyond the area of communist rule were other European lands not part of the NATO defense system—Austria and Finland being the obvious examples—which we had been assuming were safe from Soviet "protection" but where new anxieties had arisen. On the first day of the Czechoslovakia crisis, a perceptive European made the relevant comment in a NATO meeting, "The Russians have said they're serious about protecting their harem, but they haven't said how big it is."

*   *   *

The first reaction of the North Atlantic Alliance to the mounting Czech crisis before the invasion was to watch carefully but lie low. Despite the Warsaw Pact's large and obvious maneuvers, the agreed political guess (that this threat was directed against a Pact ally, not against NATO) led to agreed allied policy: scrupulously to avoid giving the Russians any Western excuse to move against Czechoslovakia.

This restraint was not, as restraint so often is, the paralysis of timidity. It was a conscious policy consensus in the North Atlantic Council. It did not save the Czechoslovaks, of course; nor was it intended to. But the policy "worked" in the sense of helping to make unbelievable the Kremlin's later attempts to pin the ideological "crimes" of the Czechoslovak leaders on dark forces of external subversion.

After the invasion, the Council's first decision was to keep on lying low—to take some minimum measures of military vigilance but not to imply by a noisy alert or mobilization that there was a sudden danger to the West. Nothing, it was felt, should be done to detract from the efforts to condemn the Soviet invasion in the U.N. Security Council.

But behind the scenes the invasion had brought into being a NATO work program of impressive and exhausting scope: a book of lessons learned about Soviet logistics and mobility and tactics, a special inquiry into the "warning" issue, a re-estimate of Soviet intentions, a complex consultation about the dampening of East-West contacts, a study on the economic implications, a revision of plans for regional arms-control proposals, and a new look at NATO's force plans in the light of the new uncertainties. The first product of the intensive daily work—"drafting by night and tearing it to pieces by day"—emerged on September 4, when NATO's Defense Planning Committee published a declaration marking the end of the "lie-low" policy. The statement reminded a suddenly attentive world of the defense-cum-détente policy formalized by NATO Ministers at their May and June meetings. Prospects for mutual force reductions having "suffered a severe setback," the Alliance members said they proposed to maintain their military capabilities, and announced a thorough assessment of NATO's forces in the light of "recent developments in Eastern Europe."

In effect, this was a pledge that there would be no reduction of forces pending comprehensive analysis and deliberate decision-making by the Council. It was needed as a stopgap policy because many of the allies were well into a process of trimming defense budgets, shaving their contributions to NATO, relaxing their readiness levels, and neglecting standards for weapons and stocks.

To shift gears, from reverse to forward, is hard enough for a single government; in an international organization the task is compounded by a factor somewhat greater than the number of its members. An international organization moves by fits and starts, and the fits are called Ministerial meetings. Western Europe's first reaction to the Czech invasion was to assume that NATO woud call a special meeting of Foreign and Defense Ministers—Chancellor Kiesinger even suggested a meeting at summit level—to stress Alliance solidarity and strengthen the defense of the West.

Other NATO nations began by looking to Washington for a

cue. But President Johnson had not given up the idea of holding a U.S.-U.S.S.R. summit before he left office; a quick indignation meeting of the Western allies might look as if they were starting with the cold war again. Moreover, before plunging into a NATO-strengthening bargain, he wanted to see whether the Europeans would back their verbal expressions of alarm with "money, marbles and chalk." So Washington passed the initiative back to the Europeans: a great gathering of NATO Ministers, I told the Council, would be useful only when each government had had time to give its allies "concrete indications" of what it thought it could do to beef up NATO. We should know the dénouement before turning on the drama.

To hear that we wanted to see the color of their money, most of our allies were not as surprised as they contrived to look. To discover that in the post-invasion atmosphere we still were acting out our dedication to détente and U.S.-Soviet summitry, even Europe's most single-minded peacemongers were frankly amazed.

For a variety of reasons, all related to their internal politics, none of the members wanted to blow the opening whistle and suggest a new target for NATO-after-Czechoslovakia. Yet most said privately that they could do more for NATO if the members asked for more to be done. The problem was to put together concrete national steps in the form of a "collective initiative" in which no member seemed to be out in front, and to which each member could respond. This was a job for the Council in Permanent Session. In time and with mutual prodding there were enough "concrete indications" of added defense efforts to justify moving up the regular December meeting of NATO Ministers.

It was a foregone conclusion that the collective Western defense system would have to be strengthened. As the meetings were held, the deficiencies unveiled, the plans for improvement laid, and the cost of alertness calculated, a wide consensus was soon evident on what kind of collective response NATO should make. (The questions of exactly who should do exactly what, for how long, at whose expense, naturally took a little longer.) Before the end of September, NATO's fourteen active defenders had decided that what was needed was not so much *more*, as *better* forces. If the Soviets were readier, NATO should be readier.

If Soviet behavior were less predictable, then NATO needed an even more flexible "flexible response" strategy, with all that implied for mobility and trained reserves and speed of reaction in a crisis.

When the Ministers finally met in mid-November, they agreed to add more than $1 billion to the plans already laid out for the two or three years just ahead, not to increase the number of divisions, squadrons and ships but to bring their manning, training, equipment and stocks closer to NATO standards. They also agreed that even this was not really enough, and set the stage for later decisions to improve quality some more. Nearly half the announced increase was contributed by Germany. The Netherlands and Italy made respectable new contributions, and all the Fourteen but one managed to do something they would not otherwise have done. The British made only a token contribution, for a special reason. They were already scheduled to increase their NATO contribution during the next few years from savings "East-of-Suez," but unfortunately for their posture in the November pledging session, most of their new contributions had been announced before the invasion of Czechoslovakia. The U.S. contribution, less than 10 per cent of the "new" effort, also understated reality: we were already committed to a massive "get well" program to fill in our own European forces and also the NATO Strategic Reserve divisions in the United States, which had been much depleted for Vietnam reinforcements.

One of the "new" actions the United States announced in November stretched the adjective a little. We promised to put up money to exercise in Europe early in 1969 the troops and air elements which had been redeployed and dual-based earlier in 1968. For budget reasons, again connected with Vietnam, the Defense Department had decided to postpone that promised exercise until much later in the year; but since we had not told our allies about this, they were a little puzzled when we took post-invasion credit for bringing these troops back when they had expected them anyhow. Late that winter the promise was fulfilled; it helped make the point that we really meant to treat these forces as in a special sense part of our European defense commitment. Unfortunately, the shortage of non-Vietnam money prevented a demonstration of how fast we could bring the dual-based forces back to Europe in an emergency. In 1963, in Exercise BIG LIFT, we had airlifted an entire division, 14,983 men and 116 tons of equipment, to Europe in 63 hours. In 1969, with modern jet aircraft, we airlifted two-thirds of a division, about 10,000 men, and got them to Europe over a period of ten days. The rest of the reassurance we had to supply with press releases.

The one holdout in the November pledging session was Canada, whose new Prime Minister, Pierre Elliott Trudeau, had already started a comprehensive defense review. In effect, he was challenging his experts and even his External Affairs and Defense Ministers to show cause why Canada should not adopt a stance toward the Alliance which would save some money by reducing Canada's commitment to the defense of Europe. Overruling the urgings of the two Ministers, tossing out the nearly unanimous advice of the relevant government advisers, side-stepping a strongly pro-NATO report by the Standing Committee on External Affairs and National Defense of the Canadian House of Commons, and disregarding urgent and in some cases emotional pleas by his European allies, Trudeau and a majority of his Cabinet decided in the spring of 1969 to cut from 10,000 to 3,500 the mechanized brigade and Air Force squadrons that had served SACEUR as a model of professional quality.

Strangely, a Canadian defection might turn out to matter more than had France's "withdrawal." Canada's forces would be gone for good from the scene of action. To be sure, the NATO defense system can get along without a few thousand men, even exceptionally good ones. But Canada's action to rid itself of foreign responsibilities was bound to be suggestive to those in U.S. politics who feel the same urge to turn inward for a while. If Ottawa started a chain reaction of which Washington was the next link, the multiplier effect might be enormous.

In a larger sense, Canada would be sorely missed in an Alliance where there is such a need to keep the transatlantic bargain from becoming a "horse and rabbits" stew. Canada's special understanding of the United States, combined with its articulately independent stance, have enabled a series of unusually effective representatives at NATO to play a role altogether out of proportion to their government's defense spending. They have helped give respectability to the word "Atlantic." Nor is it clear that pulling away from NATO helps Canada accomplish the avowed purpose of Trudeau's policy: to bolster its "sovereignty" vis-à-vis the large and importunate neighbor to the south. The more Canada isolates itself with the United States in a North American twosome, the more Canada deprives itself of the countervailing weight of the European allies in balancing the scales with the United States.

*   *   *

The disparity in power between Europe and America—the anomaly that nearly 300,000,000 Western Europeans produce only half as much goods and services and can afford to spend only one-fifth as much on their defense as 200,000,000 Americans —had long been a source of dissatisfaction on both banks of the "Atlantic river." We have just seen how the American malaise spurs efforts to withdraw U.S. forces from Europe. Nevertheless, Europeans can resent being the weaker partner just as much as Americans can resent being the stronger one.

There was during the 1960s a growing feeling in Europe that the European members of NATO should combine their efforts for defense and not remain forever a dependency of the Pentagon. If this feeling had been operational, it would have led to a massive rise in European defense spending and a United States of Europe with its own nuclear arms. No responsible politician in Europe wanted to spend that kind of money, nor was there the remotest chance for popular support in doing so. A number of less responsible politicians, however, were needling their constituents about how terrible it was to depend on American weapons and decisions, without proposing the hard work and financial sacrifice a more independent defense posture would entail. A fortiori, no one in Europe was seriously suggesting a European nuclear force, which would be far more expensive than any marginal increases in conventional effort. In four years in Europe, I often read about European nuclear forces in newspapers and the speeches of opposition politicians, but I never met a responsible member of a European government who gave the notion the time of day.

Nevertheless the burning sensation remained, and some Europeans looking for ointment found it in the idea that Europeans should get together within the framework of NATO—that would be doing something European, without actually spending any more money. This idea first was called the European "caucus," but that Algonquian word connoted smoke-filled rooms at some of the more sordid moments in American political history and was quickly suppressed in favor of a European entity, identity, personality, or voice.

As often in politics, the purposes were plural. Some Europeans reasoned that a concerted European influence would help ensure that the United States would maintain its troop levels in Europe and consult on important matters affecting European interests, like the U.S.-Soviet talks on strategic arms control. Other Europeans, notably the British, together with some Americans, were assuming the United States would reduce its military presence in Europe over the next few years and felt that the European members of the Alliance must therefore become more self-reliant by cooperating more closely with each other in NATO defense matters. One of the prime motivations was related to the politics of European integration: advocates of British entry into the Common Market saw the NATO caucus as a backdoor way of keeping some trans-Channel dialogue going with Europeans other than the French, while General de Gaulle had his foot firmly planted against opening the front door. Still other Europeans, including most German leaders, did not warm to the caucus idea at all; the French would be annoyed, they thought, and the United States would take greater European cooperation on defense matters as a welcome excuse to reduce American commitments.

In the fall of 1968 Denis Healey, the British Secretary of State for Defense, started a series of "Eurodinners" among the Defense Ministers. (The Gaullist Defense Minister Pierre Messmer, was politely invited to the first one but, to Healey's undisguised relief, declined.) Staff work between dinners was done at afternoon "Euroteas" among Ambassadors at NATO. The participants in these consultative repasts did manage to develop a common European view on some NATO matters, though the Germans ruled off the course subjects on which European caucusing would offend either France or the United States. The most effective caucus subject was Canada's 1969 troop withdrawal plan; with U.S. encouragement, the European Ministers parceled out arguments and debating assignments, and fired a well-coordinated salvo at the Canadian Defense Minister (who had himself fought against the Trudeau policy in his own Cabinet) in the toughest talk I have ever heard in an international meeting.

In general, the American posture has been to encourage the Europeans to get together, but they naturally find it easier to agree about what the United States should do than to agree on ways they themselves could pick up a bigger share of the load. Sometimes this has served a useful purpose. When President Nixon, in one of his first personal messages to European leaders, asked them whether they wanted another American general to succeed General Lyman Lemnitzer as SACEUR, the Europeans consulted each other through the Brussels caucus, and returned with a prompt and unanimous endorsement of General Andrew Goodpaster as the new Supreme Commander for Europe. But if the primary function of the European voice is to "talk back to teacher," as Healey once frankly put it, and Europeans find European defense cooperation too touchy a topic, the voice will increasingly grate on American ears and harm, not help, the efforts of those in Washington who want the United States to continue to choose the way of partnership.

Chapter VII

The Management of Détente

The word is détente, French for "relaxation." East and West in Europe, it is used as shorthand for improvement in East-West relations. Everybody talks about détente and nobody is relaxed.

There was a time, fading into history now with the cold war, when governments in the West were fearful of too much contact with the communist-run East, worried about their own communist politicians acting as agents of a foreign power, even afraid that communism might seem dangerously dynamic and attractive to their peoples. For many years—it is foolish to be precise about historical periods—two sides of divided Europe faced each other in almost instinctive, automatic hostility. This reflected, and in turn inflated, the sense of military insecurity on both sides. To the Western allies, the Soviets and their satellite states seemed to have more conventional arms than could possibly be needed except to threaten NATO; to the Soviets, the United States no doubt seemed to possess more nuclear power than it could possibly need except for blackmailing them and keeping America's allies in line. As the Soviet nuclear program proceeded successfully and NATO turned to modernizing its conventional forces, there came to be a clear, tested, and stable stalemate in arms and political determination. Over time, attitudes began to change.

Things changed inside the Soviet Union. The terror became less oppressive. The censorship was alternately eased and tightened, permitting some freedom of expression, though dissenting writers still wound up in jail. The technicians became more pragmatic, the agricultural economists more sensible, the managers of industry less allergic to incentives and even competition. The leaders became more cautious, especially after their third ultimatum over Berlin petered out and the battle of wills over the missiles in Cuba was lost.

Things changed in the relationship between the East European states and the Soviet Union. As the Stalinist grip over the Soviet people loosened a bit, so did the Kremlin's grip over the peoples of Poland, Czechoslovakia, Hungary, Bulgaria, and Rumania. The old itch to be independent began to be felt, even within the communist regimes. The old spirit of nationalism, useful for this purpose but foreboding for the future, began to return. Within the "communist world," what was once thought to be a monolithic structure became so fractured that we reached for our morning papers to see which splinter of the communist church was accusing which other faction of revisionism, splittism, dogmatism, capitalism, or bourgeoisification of the proletariat. On the long, tense border with China, the Soviets faced dozens of incidents a month; looking south and east, they could hardly rejoice in seeing so close a neighbor so wracked with dissension, so dedicated to violence as a way of life and government.

Meanwhile Western Europe grew. In spite of obstacles, frustrations, throw-backs, defections and disappointments, it passed the point of no return in building a market of continental size. With the sense of growing prosperity and guaranteed protection came a deepening resentment of the congestion, the pollution, and the bureaucratic conformity that seem to be the aftermath of affluence. Student turbulence and widespread strikes slowed economies, fed inflationary pressure, frightened the middle classes, threatened half a dozen governments, and prepared the downfall of de Gaulle in France.

The confluence of these tides of change created a new kind of East-West stalemate—unclear, untested, unstable, and subject to violence of internal origin. Yet the mood in the West was increasingly one of impatience with the notion that Europeans could ever fight each other again, a mood of suppressed expectation and anxious search for signs of a turning point that would convert détente from a slogan to a condition. The cold war came to seem an unattractive bore. Each in its own style, the governments of the Atlantic Alliance opened wider relations with the Soviet Union and the countries of Eastern Europe through trade, through exchanges of students and professors and musicians and dancers, through thousands of conversations between journalists, scientists, experts on housing and coal and transportation and agriculture—and more cautiously, between ministers of government.

As the situation changed, the North Atlantic Alliance, which was one of the prime instruments of that change, began to build on top of its military deterrent an allied search for a political détente with the Soviets. A new political phase of NATO had begun.

There was nothing relaxing about it. In one meeting of the North Atlantic Council, I suggested only half in jest that when translating "détente" into English we should avoid the word "relaxation"; we would do better to adapt the Clausewitz cliché and define détente as "the continuation of tension by other means." Driving holes through an increasingly porous Iron Curtain had quite different effects from those intended on either side. What started in the West as sentimental popular yearning for some better kind of peace than a bristling military confrontation appeared to the Soviet rulers as a hard-line Western effort to subvert their system by osmosis. The doctrine of peaceful coexistence, which started as a Kremlin ploy to split the Western Alliance, turned out to be a better way to undermine "socialist solidarity" in Eastern Europe than shouting anti-communist polemics at it had ever been.

*   *   *

During the 1960s the main source of kinetic energy in East-West relations was not coexistence talk in the East but wish-thinking in the West. By what means to relax with the communists, or to continue the tensions with them, has for several years now been a central foreign-policy issue in the domestic politics of almost every Western nation. In the NATO countries a major politician, in or out of office, must be seen as potential peacemaker or he is dead.

That is why, in the year just prior to the invasion of Czechoslovakia, about one hundred high-level political visits pierced the Curtain. General de Gaulle led the parade with a royal tour of the Soviet Union in the summer of 1966, a visit to Warsaw in 1967, and one to Bucharest in May 1968—where he was when the Latin Quarter erupted back home in Paris. Soviet Premier Kosygin returned de Gaulle's visit without delay; six months after they parted at the Vnukovo airport, Kosygin was getting a 101-gun salute (usually reserved for Chiefs of State) at Orly airport near Paris.

De Gaulle had qualified as a Soviet interlocutor by pulling out of the NATO defense system, and the Russians treated him like royalty. The French President spoke from the Moscow City Hall balcony used by Lenin; he became the first Westerner since Napoleon to stay at the Kremlin, and the first ever to witness the launching of a Cosmos satellite (No. 122) from the Soviet space center at Baikonur. But the Soviet leaders were careful not to do anything that implied they regarded de Gaulle as representing the West as a whole. When it comes to discussing the future of Germany or the limitation of armaments, they knew they had to deal with the whole West, preferably (from their standpoint, not necessarily from ours) through Washington.

The consolation prize was a series of Franco-Soviet agreements about technological cooperation, including potentially far-reaching cooperation in satellite communications, television, and atomic energy. Since the Russians had not finally decided whether to fight or join the global communications satellite program based on U.S. technology, the arrangements with France dragged on interminably. More than two years after de Gaulle's visit to Russia a French official told me that all the technical arrangements supposedly agreed then had bogged down through delays on the Soviet side. Nevertheless, a French newspaper reader or television viewer was left with the impression that his country had cashed in its independence from NATO for a special relationship with the Soviet Union and was leading the parade toward détente in Europe. And it is of impressions, not underlying facts, that short-run politics is made.

Meanwhile the Socialists in Bonn were dragging their Christian Democratic coalition partners toward a made-in-Germany peace initiative of their own. Without much notice to their allies in NATO, and sometimes without clearance with their own Chancellor, Foreign Minister Willy Brandt and Herbert Wehner, the Minister for All-German Affairs, were launching East-West trial balloons with impressive frequency. One was a proposal for the mutual renunciation of force, an old idea of John Foster Dulles; for twenty years its revival has been good for a one-day headline. Another was a series of special efforts to widen the exchange of people and goods between the two parts of Germany, and between East and West Berlin.

The most serious, and initially the most successful, German effort was designed to re-establish diplomatic relations with the nations of Eastern Europe. (The Soviet Union, though itself recognizing the Federal Republic of Germany, had been reluctant to see its Warsaw Pact partners do so). As bait, Brandt proposed to abandon the Hallstein Doctrine by which the Federal Republic had for many years refused to have diplomatic intercourse with any nation which recognized the East German regime that called itself the German Democratic Republic; the abandonment had to be gradual, because some powerful members of the Bonn coalition had not yet decided the Hallstein Doctrine had outlived its usefulness.

Germany's *Ostpolitik*, or Eastern policy, produced an enormous reaction in Eastern Europe. Rumania, which likes the role of the Warsaw Pact member with the most independent foreign policy, had its own reasons for taking up Bonn's offer early in 1967. The strong reaction from Moscow, and of course from East Berlin, made the other Warsaw Pact states draw back from following suit, though Yugoslavia, whose rulers had always followed their own interests, moved toward renewing relations with the Federal Republic, broken by the latter in 1957. The German drive was slowed, but not stopped. Brandt encouraged the Poles to think hard by announcing (at a Socialist Party conclave, not as a government statement) that he thought the Oder-Neisse border could be made permanent. And Czechoslovakia, under its new regime in 1968, was getting ready to negotiate with Bonn when the ax fell in August.

The Czech crisis may have been in part a Soviet reaction to the Federal Republic's diplomatic efforts in its front yard. At first the Soviets were pleased to see the German Foreign Minister knocking holes in the Hallstein Doctrine; that was a victory for the communist way of solving the "German question," which is to confirm the juridical existence and equality of two Germanies—what every trained Soviet diplomat calls "recognizing reality." But beyond the destruction of the Hallstein Doctrine the way was not so clear or so attractive to the Kremlin: the West Germans might well isolate the East Germans from their Warsaw Pact allies by practicing "discriminatory détente" in reverse.

In retrospect, thoughtful and intelligent German leaders believe that the Federal Republic miscalculated both the method and the pace of their 1967–68 *Ostpolitik*: it was too German, and it went too far too fast. Willy Brandt deliberately pursued the policy as an independent German initiative with a minimum of NATO consultation partly because he foresaw that the allies, especially the French, might be reluctant to see Germany competing in the race for détente, and partly, perhaps, because he was operating beyond the consensus in his own government. To the German Socialists, the vigorous pursuit of détente seemed the best way to bid for electoral victory in 1969 and thus extricate themselves from their junior partnership with the Christian Democrats in a "Grand" but uncomfortable coalition. One of Italy's most perceptive analysts gave the verdict shortly after the Czech invasion: "It was a mistake for the *Ostpolitik* to be German; it should have been a common Western policy."

Political leaders in the other continental members of the North Atlantic Alliance were equally anxious to make peace with the communists; indeed, each fresh initiative by one Western country put pressure on the others to try harder. The Italians were quite frank about their motivation: whenever they made a gesture or planned a trip, their diplomats would say with a Mediterranean shrug that their allies would certainly understand the domestic reasons for their action. Rumania was a special target of Roman efforts, and vice versa; hardly a month went by, during this period, without a public reminder of their common Latin heritage. The Belgian Foreign Minister, Pierre Harmel, filling with skill and dignity the enormous shoes of Paul-Henri Spaak, made himself a symbol of détente—which also helped him survive the frequent and complex mutations in Belgian coalition politics. He developed, for example, a special relationship with Poland; when the Czech crisis blew, he was negotiating with the Poles an agreed paper on disarmament. Dr. Joseph Luns, the permanent Foreign Minister of The Netherlands, had long been regarded as the toughest and staunchest of cold warriors. But faced with a restive Left at home and the détente politics of his Benelux colleague in Brussels, Luns suddenly decided to bring to life, by joining it, the Group of Nine which thus became Ten—an informal small-country forum of three NATO countries, three Warsaw Pact members, and four European neutrals.

Denmark's Premier, Jens Otto Krag, trying to keep his left-of-center party in office, mistakenly thought his main threat was from the pacifist Left and became one of the most expansive players of détente politics. Elections proved otherwise, and a coalition of more conservative parties took over; but faced with crossfire from Krag in opposition, the new Cabinet soon got the hang of making public peace-making gestures of its own. Even in Norway, which traditionally keeps its pacifist predilections well within a framework of allied cooperation, it seemed natural for Otto Grieg Tidemand, a conservative Defense Minister, to visit Moscow and hobnob with his opposite number Marshal A. A. Grechko. Tidemand's bluff candor was heard with respect, but the absence of follow-up suggests that the Soviets did not see much chance to get the sensible Norwegians working for their notion of détente.

Both Prime Minister Harold Wilson and would-be Prime Minister Edward Heath have visited Moscow, as often as opportunity affords, to push disarmament, to suggest an East-West "code of conduct," to offer their good offices on Vietnam and the Middle East. On one return visit Soviet Premier Aleksei Kosygin showed that he too had been studying the Western game of détente politics. Speaking on British television—and before broaching his subject with the British government—Kosygin proposed a Treaty of Friendship between the Soviet Union and the United Kingdom. Given the hearty appetite for peace gestures on their own Left, the leaders of British Labour could hardly rap their Russian visitor's knuckles, so they publicly agreed to negotiate about friendship.

The Foreign Office was of course not anxious to concede to its friends abroad that the usually skillful British had been "had" by an ancient political trick. It therefore compounded the difficulty by exhibiting an embarrassed reluctance to consult in the North Atlantic Council about the content of such a treaty. Britain's European allies were understandably upset. Several of them had already rebuffed similar approaches from the Soviets as exercises in political symbolism without real content; and the Germans, who had not been offered a Friendship Treaty, promptly scored the tactic as "discriminatory détente" designed not to improve East-West relations but to drive a wedge between the Federal Republic and its allies. In time the British, having made clear to their own people that they dearly wanted friendship with the Soviets but the details were a little complicated, turned their Foreign Office experts loose to draft a treaty and demonstrated in the Council that any text they bought would be hortatory, harmless, and consistent with their NATO obligations.

Since the Soviets had known that all along, the "negotiation" of the "treaty" ran quietly out into the sands of diplomatic procedure, and nothing more was heard of the project. The outcome was no great surprise to Harold Wilson either. He could have told Kosygin from the outset that there was no nourishment in the idea. But he had to pretend to welcome it, for fear of looking like a cold warrior to his own domestic constituency. It was a good example of "détente politics" at work. British contributions to the dialogue on disarmament often have the same air of international unreality combined with domestic practicality. In the summer of 1968, just two months after anti-war protestors had demonstrated against the production of chemical and biological agents at Porton Down in Wiltshire, a British Minister traveled to Geneva to propose a sweeping and improbable East-West agreement on chemical and biological warfare.

Washington is no less susceptible than Paris, Bonn, or London to the lure of détente politics. At his first NATO meeting President Nixon repeated what he had said during his electoral campaign and in his inaugural address: "We are ending a period of confrontation and entering an era of negotiation." But he reminded the Foreign Ministers that although the road to popularity in U.S. politics would be a quick summit meeting, some careful planning and intensive NATO consultation was first in order. Doubtless he remembered the hopes and letdowns of the Eisenhower administration and had meanwhile watched the interaction of peace with politics during the Kennedy-Johnson years.

The "spirit of Camp David," when President Eisenhower had Nikita Khrushchev as a weekend guest in 1959 at his retreat in the Maryland hills, came to grief in the abortive summit meeting in Paris in 1960 because of the thoughtless timing and failure of a U-2 reconnaissance flight over Russia. President Kennedy had met with Khrushchev in Vienna in 1961 and, despite subsequent high tension over Berlin and Russian missiles in Cuba, produced in his June 1963 speech at American University a rounded rationale for a U.S. policy of unremitting efforts to negotiate with the Soviet Union. President Johnson was no less ambitious than his predecessors to make a breakthrough in relations with the Russians; he met with Premier Kosygin at Glassboro, N.J., in 1967, and his administration projected the imagery of "bridge-building" and "peaceful engagement" to match the rhetoric of "peaceful coexistence."

When President Nixon visited Rumania in August 1969, he described American policy with the same pragmatic preference for diversity that John F. Kennedy had used. The nations, he told welcomers at the Bucharest airport, must be prepared "to see the world as it is—a world of different races, of different nations, of different social systems—a real world, where many interests divide

men and many unite them. . . . nations can have widely different
internal orders and live in peace."

*   *   *

In 1969 the expression of such sentiments was quite compatible
with strong support for the North Atlantic Alliance, because
nearly every one had learned the lesson that defense and détente
have to be two parts of the same Western policy. The lesson had
not been easy to learn. Three years earlier there had been no such
clarity; indeed, by the autumn of 1966 the hopes for détente
were a clear and present danger to the existence of NATO.
France's defection was only the most obvious symptom of a per-
vasive psychosis: the self-induced pox of détente fever was visible
all over Western Europe, and in North America too. Responsible
editors and powerful politicians were predicting an imminent
period of East-West relaxation and wondering out loud whether
that did not mean an end to the period of defense effort. Finance
Ministers and parliamentarians were chopping at military spending, citing the improbability of the war NATO was preparing for,
and reasoning that reductions in Western defense budgets would
persuade the East to do likewise. Some political leaders were even
leery of being seen at NATO meetings unless they were assured
that the outcome would feature predictions of peace with the
Soviets. And the competition among them for peacemaking
laurels was already so intense that in the North Atlantic Council,
first in private and then in public, we began to discuss a whole
new function for the Alliance, the management of détente.

The coordination of members' foreign policies, especially in
matters directly affecting their security, had always been implicit
in the Treaty, inherent in the establishment of a permanent
political Council, and explicit in the legislative history of Alliance
consultation, sketched in Chapter 2. The Council, says the NATO
Handbook in cleared and careful prose, "is playing an indispensable daily role as a forum and clearing house for the widest possible consultation between member governments." But political
consultation had never been the Council's main business; until
the mid-1960s the Permanent Representatives spent most of their

time serving as the board of directors of the NATO defense system, itself a full-time job.

Most of the time, not enough was happening, or deemed likely to happen, in East-West relations to justify extensive policy planning by the allies as a group. It is true that the roads to the quietly abortive 1959 Four-Power meeting on Germany in Geneva, and to the spectacularly abortive 1960 summit in Paris, were paved with consultation. During the Berlin crisis of 1961 the Council was currently informed of policies developed in direct negotiations with Bonn by the United States, Britain, and France, which still have special responsibilities resulting from the Second World War. Disarmament talks, too, were reported to the Council and responsibly discussed. But there was little international staffwork in NATO on these subjects, and the weekly meetings of the Committee of Political Advisers featured the desultory exchange of after-the-fact information among comparatively junior officials. Before the late 1960s, there were not many examples of the allies negotiating a common approach to political issues of vital interest.

Nevertheless, by 1966 détente had to be taken seriously, at least as a prime mover in the politics of the Alliance. Canada and other members had been pushing for a full-blown self-study in NATO, and the idea quite suddenly caught on. In planning the December Ministerial meeting, several of the delegations, including our own, decided that a major stock-taking was the only way to stop the slide in defense spending, develop a détente-management system, and avoid handing the Soviets by political default the mastery of Europe's future which they had not been able to gain by force or pressure.

The U.S. aims at this time were rather simple: to keep NATO's deterrent credible enough so that the Soviets would have to negotiate about the future of Europe and not merely await Western decisions to melt down the "NATO shield"; and to develop a system of much closer consultation, so that in any negotiations the Soviets and their friends would not have the option of playing the allies off against each other. I have told the story of a precarious success in keeping the major allies, notably our own government in Washington, from melting their defenses in the warmth of détente. The attempt to beef up political consultation at first presented an even more discouraging picture, but in the end worked out better than any of us directly involved would have predicted.

We faced some formidable obstacles. There was of course the inherent dilemma of Alliance consultation, the two-faced reluctance of every sovereign government to admit that its own efforts at "détente politics" needed coordinating, while strongly advocating "before and during" consultation by other allies. But in consulting about the political future of Europe, there were three special hurdles to clear.

First, some of the more "European" Western Europeans honestly preferred a peacemaking pattern in which they got together in the first instance with the East Europeans without undue interference from their transatlantic allies. The United States would of course have to ratify the ultimate European settlement, and guarantee it militarily too; no combination of European states, no matter how closely integrated, was a match for Russian nuclear power. But, they asked, did the Americans (and by implication the Canadians) really have to be in on the initial negotiations? Whenever the question surfaced, my instructions were to answer with an unambiguous Yes; as Dean Acheson had put it years before, the United States is (among other things) a European power.

Second, there was the sticky problem of Three-Power responsibilities for the ultimate settlement in Germany and Berlin. The French were reluctant to consult with any allies outside the Four (the United States, Britain, France, and the Federal Republic of Germany), which had organized for the purpose regular meetings of their diplomatic representatives in Bonn. The German tendency to play *Ostpolitik* close to the chest, and the natural instinct of American and British experts on Germany to protect the Germans from criticism by their NATO allies, inhibit timely consultations with the other eleven allies on issues affecting Germany and Berlin; and nearly every question about the future of Europe is at bottom an issue about Germany and Berlin.

The *pas de deux* between the big Four and the other Eleven is danced several times a year on one issue or another. Whenever

Foreign Ministers get together for a NATO meeting, another warning has to be emitted about Berlin. Back in 1958 the Council had endorsed the right of the three Western Powers to remain in Berlin (this was just after Khrushchev had tried to terminate the Four-Power agreement on the status of the already divided city); the Eleven had thereby accepted by implication that if the Three, plus West Germany, got into a fight over Berlin the Eleven would be at their allies' side even though Berlin is not strictly speaking in the NATO defense perimeter. Now, whenever the Foreign Ministers meet, the Four want the Eleven to take that pledge again, and the Eleven exact in return another pledge from the Four that they will be good about Germany/Berlin consultations. Both groups take the pledge with some mental reservation and purpose of evasion.

Third, the participation of France in intimate political consultations was a puzzle. De Gaulle had just pulled out of NATO's military arrangements under conditions which other participants in the transatlantic bargain saw as unilateral violation of pacts and presumptions. France remained a partner in political consultation and was still represented in the North Atlantic Council; by the irony of alphabetical rotation, Couve de Murville was Honorary President of the Council the year after the French defection. None of the allies wanted to push France out of any activities in which it was willing to participate, however reluctantly. (During this period I referred in a meeting to "the accelerating irrelevance of France" in NATO operations, a not inaccurate description of reality at that moment in time. I was prepared for an icy reaction from the Quai d'Orsay, but not for the defense of French relevance that several of France's bitterest continental critics felt it necessary to put forward in reply.) Yet France did remain, even on political matters, the most reluctant ally, and there was real danger of a bottleneck to all consultation just as changes in military strategy had been frozen for years by French objection.

The French delegation to the Council was headed during this period by a succession of skillful and sensitive Ambassadors— Pierre de Leusse, Roger Seydoux, and Jacques Kosciusko-Morizet. Their efforts to square some degree of political cooperation with their oracular instructions from the Élysée Palace must have been exacting tests of intestinal fortitude. But in the fall of 1966 the Fourteen had one great tactical advantage in dealings with Paris: while the standing policy of General de Gaulle was not to agree to anything that smacked of "collective policy" in the Alliance, he was preparing that season to renew the battle with his Common Market partners about British entry, and clearly did not want to reopen a second front with NATO.

*   *   *

This, then, was the climate in which the North Atlantic Council decided to conduct a Study of the Future Tasks of the Alliance. In some international organizations the word "study" means a rational piece of analytical paper, or even an article for an academic journal. In NATO, "study" is a euphemism for a highly practical negotiation about the degree to which governments are going to act in common. A Study of the Future Tasks of the Alliance, set in motion just two and a half years before the date when nations could legally give notice of withdrawal, was therefore highly significant business. To a majority of member governments, facing (they then thought) domestic political crises about the continuation of their association with the Alliance system beyond its twentieth year, such a "study" was high politics.

Writing "terms of reference" for a study does not sound like exciting work. But the argument over how to get this study started brought to a head three interesting and far-reaching policy questions: Should not the European members form a caucus within the Atlantic Alliance? Would the French defect from the political work of the Alliance too? In studying the Alliance's horoscope, was the Council supposed to decide *whether* or merely *how* to carry on with the transatlantic bargain?

We have seen in an earlier chapter how strong and how vague is the notion that the Europeans should get together in dealing with their own defense, or at least in dealing with their transatlantic ally. In its first public appearance, sponsored not by a British Defense Minister in 1968, but by a Belgian Foreign Minister in 1966, the "European caucus" idea was even vaguer. When Pierre Harmel first started talking about what came to be known as the "Harmel Plan," he was talking not about the transatlantic bargain but about the need to organize in "caucus" the European bargainers. Some new European solidarity, he thought, should be the centerpiece of NATO's Study of Future Tasks.

The French, already locked in battle with their neighbors about European economic institutions, had no stomach for another European entity to wrangle with. The United States and also Canada, while welcoming the notion that Europeans might get together and do more (enabling us to do less), did not regard a European caucus as the specific remedy to restore to health an Atlantic Alliance ill with détente fever. In negotiations with the French and American delegations (in which Eugene Rostow, our commuting Undersecretary of State for Political Affairs, played a cheerful part), Harmel ultimately agreed to broaden the focus; it was, indeed, hard to find the original European caucus idea in the Study of Future Tasks, which came to be known as the "Harmel exercise."

In a way, the most important decision about the Harmel exercise was taken before the "study" even began. With some support from those (Canadians, Danes, some Belgians, and Italians) who wanted to make sure at any cost that the French cooperated at least in NATO's political work, the French wanted to "study" (read, "negotiate about") whether the Alliance had a future. But others, including the Germans, British, and Americans, were determined to prejudice the study from the outset in the direction of the continuing need for something very like NATO.

What settled this issue in the end was French reluctance to break with their European allies in NATO while arguing with them on Common Market issues, and a parallel reluctance to be seen fighting with Washington, which was no longer good public relations back in France. In the end the French delegation sold its Paris supervisors on the notion that a "study" was, after all, just an academic excursion and not a serious diplomatic negotiation. During the year that followed, that reasoning came back to haunt the French negotiators. The Harmel *Report* took shape as a major declaration of long-term Alliance policy, and the Quai d'Orsay began to mutter about a double-cross: "We thought this was just going to be a *study*."

The "study" was set in motion December 16, 1966, by a Resolution of the North Atlantic Council—a procedure unusual enough to be solemn. Proposed by M. Harmel after much redrafting behind the scenes, it was passed unanimously, but not before every word, in two languages, was parsed and juggled and twisted into place. Even the title of the study was a policy question. If the "Future of the Alliance" had been studied that would have implied doubt about continuation of the Alliance beyond 1969. "Future Tasks" assumed that NATO would survive its twentieth birthday, and called only its functions and priorities into question.

The Resolution told the Permanent Council "to undertake a broad analysis of international developments since the signing of the North Atlantic Treaty"—this, to give the lie to those who were saying NATO did not know 1966 was not 1949—and "to determine the influence of such developments on the Alliance and to identify the tasks which lie before it, in order to strengthen the Alliance as a factor of durable peace." The essence of the final outcome was already contained in that purpose clause: the Alliance was to be strengthened, and was itself to assume responsibility for making a durable peace.

In order to let some fresh air into the sometimes too intimate circle of NATO consulters, the Permanent Council then established a Special Group, to which some governments sent political-level representatives from capitals, among them Brandt's protégé Klaus Schuetz, soon to be Mayor of Berlin, Minister of State Fred Mulley from London, and Eugene Rostow from Washington. Four subgroups, supposedly working without strict instructions from governments, were chaired by "independent" Rapporteurs: Schuetz and a British career diplomat, J. H. A. Watson, jointly for "East-West Relations," Grand Old Man Paul-Henri Spaak of Belgium for "Inter Allied Relations," Foy Kohler (who had just returned to Washington from five years as U.S. Ambassador to Moscow) for "General Defense Policy," and Professor C. L. Patijn of the University of Utrecht on "Relations With

Other Countries," which meant countries outside the NATO-Warsaw Pact confrontation.

It was an instructive experiment. The idea was to provide irresponsible inputs into a responsible process of policy planning. In general, where the inputs reflected the views of major governments they made a major contribution, and where they did not they did not. Kohler's report made a persuasive case for gluing defense and détente together, rather than considering defense as required in one time-period and détente in another. Kohler and his staff also provided the first full rationale for a major effort by NATO in the arms control field, suggesting more intensive consultation on Western disarmament positions, thinking of arms control as the other side of the coin of NATO force planning, and using some of the same analytical people and techniques for the purpose. In summary form, the Kohler paper found its way into the eventual Harmel *Report*.

The Schuetz-Watson paper was especially notable for its softened German line on East-West relations; as things turned out, it was a trial balloon for the *Ostpolitik*. It, too, was echoed in the final document. Professor Patijn's report advocated much more European involvement in world-wide problems of security, order, and economic development; it was harmonious music to American ears but sounded so dissonant and modernistic in Europe-centered Europe that it was never heard of again. M. Spaak, who had been Prime Minister and Foreign Minister of Belgium, President of the U.N. General Assembly, and Secretary General of NATO, devoted his report to berating General de Gaulle for stalling the growth of the European Communities. It was no more than what everybody was saying privately; but the French government objected strongly to being belabored about its Common Market toward the attitudes in a NATO document, even in Spaak's impeccable French. Ultimately, and mainly for this reason, none of the Rapporteurs' four reports was published. In multilateral diplomacy, as in other forms of politics, boldness and candor are welcome exceptions, but caution and consent are the rule.

After months of negotiations, the *Report on the Future Tasks of the Alliance* was presented to Ministers in December 1967. In a last minute switch, the French delegation not only approved the *Report* but withdrew earlier objections to its public release. After saluting the changes in the world and in East-West relations, the Harmel *Report* established what later came to be known as the "two pillar" doctrine of defense-cum-détente:

> The Atlantic Alliance has two main functions. Its first function is to maintain adequate military strength and political solidarity to deter aggression and other forms of pressure and to defend the territory of member countries if aggression should occur. Since its inception, the Alliance has successfully fulfilled this task. But the possibility of a crisis cannot be excluded as long as the central political issues in Europe, first and foremost the German question, remain unsolved. Moreover, the situation of instability and uncertainty still precludes a balanced reduction of military forces. Under these conditions, the Allies will maintain as necessary, a suitable military capability to assure the balance of forces, thereby creating a climate of stability, security and confidence.
>
> In this climate the Alliance can carry out its second function, to pursue the search for progress towards a more stable relationship in which the underlying political issues can be solved. Military security and a policy of détente are not contradictory but complementary. Collective defense is a stabilizing factor in world politics. It is a necessary condition for effective policies directed towards a greater relaxation of tensions. The way to peace and stability in Europe rests in particular on the use of the Alliance constructively in the interest of détente. The participation of the USSR and the USA will be necessary to achieve a settlement of the political problems in Europe.

The *Report* then tried, as its predecessors had done in 1951 and 1956, to square the circle of consultation, the double-ended result of which has been quoted in Chapter 2. After putting the emphasis on Germany as the key to European peace, the *Report* tried to make sure nobody missed the point that the North Atlantic Alliance was now in the peacemaking business:

> . . . the Allies are resolved to direct their energies to this purpose [a European settlement] by realistic measures designed to further a détente in East-West relations. The relaxation of tensions is not the final goal but is part of a long-term process to promote better relations and to foster a European settlement. The ultimate political purpose of the Alliance is to achieve a just and lasting peaceful order in Europe accompanied by appropriate security guarantees.

Finally, the *Report* recommended, and fifteen governments adopted, a work program. "The problem of German reunification and its relationship to a European settlement" would engage first the responsibility of the Western Three plus the Federal Republic, but "the other allies will continue to have their views considered in timely discussions . . . about Western policy." All the allies, not just the Four, would work on the wider issue of a European settlement. Nothing definitive was said about how peace would be negotiated if it turned out to be negotiable; the closest the *Report* got to this ticklish topic is a pallid sentence that almost caused a French walkout: "Certain subjects, of course, require by their very nature a multilateral solution." "Studies" (read, policy negotiations) of "disarmament and practical arms control measures . . . will be intensified." The Mediterranean, as we have seen, was deemed worthy of special attention on the defense side. And the rest of the world, said the Alliance without conviction, should not be forgotten.

Chapter VIII

The Politics of Peacemaking

Nineteen sixty-eight thus started as a promising year for détente in Europe. The Western Alliance was so obviously anxious to move beyond static peacekeeping to dynamic peacemaking that in the Norwegian Storting an antimilitaristic Left could without embarrassment join a Conservative government in passing a pro-NATO measure by a vote of 144 to 6. The West watched the drama of liberalization in Czechoslovakia with rapt attention; but the Soviet leaders seemed to be concentrating on political moves to limit the damage, and few experts and fewer statesmen and journalists thought the troop movements around the Czech border were more than a familiar tactic of political pressure; Budapest 1956 was regarded as one of a kind. In June at their Reykjavik meeting, NATO's Foreign Ministers invited the Soviets and their Warsaw Pact allies to negotiate about mutual and balanced force reductions in Europe, but prudently also repeated their determination to maintain NATO's defensive capability until something better came along.

By the third week in August the allies were mostly relaxing on the beaches, in the mountains, and in their chancelleries too. The Mayor of Moscow was in The Hague; the Red Army choir was about to entertain in the concert halls of England; the University of Minnesota Band was practicing for its trip to the U.S.S.R. John F. Kennedy Airport was braced for the second ceremonial Aeroflot flight, commencement of the new nonstop service between Moscow and New York. In Moscow, carpenters were hammering together a big Italian trade fair. And in Washington, the White House was mimeographing a press release about the agreed time and place for a summit meeting. The Western democracies, their competitive spirit aroused, had dipped their toes in "coexistence" and found they could readily swim in it.

Then the "Warsaw Five" moved into Czechoslovakia. The Soviet leaders were no longer so sure that in an environment of competitive coexistence they could stay afloat themselves.

Until that moment, most of us were holding in our heads two propositions now clearly perceived as contradictory: first, that the Czechoslovak program of liberalized communism would in the long run be fatal to the Soviet system; and second, that the Soviets would inveigh but not invade. The experts and intelligence analysts soon testified that the Russian move was perfectly rational and indeed inevitable from the Soviet point of view. Being professionals, most of them could even point to passages in their own writings which "did not exclude" an invasion. But the truth is that very few Europeans or Americans can honestly say they correctly predicted this enormous event, which called into question the fundamental assumption of loosening-by-osmosis. Perhaps Western experts should be excused for underrating the Soviets' will to use force in Czechoslovakia; so did Ceaucescu of Rumania and Tito of Yugoslavia, not to mention Alexander Dubček.

Why did the Russians do it? They evidently decided, after trying for seven months to dissuade Dubček & Co. from going too far, that their hold on the Warsaw Pact countries had to have an overriding priority—ahead of East-West relations in Europe, ahead of Soviet-American relations, even ahead of Russian leadership in the world communist movement.

The doctrinal defense of the invasion went far beyond the act itself. Later attributed to Party Chairman Brezhnev, it leans heavily on the notion that relations among states of the "socialist commonwealth" are a kind of domestic politics which are nobody else's business.

"The defense of socialism in Czechoslovakia is not only the internal affair of that country," said *Pravda* on August 22. "Can a country wrested from the socialist community really safeguard its genuine sovereignty?" asked *Izvestiia* on August 24. Sovereignty had been collectivized, at least for the purpose of justifying, *ex post facto*, the invasion and occupation of Czechoslovakia. Sovereignty, as preached and practiced by unidentified anti-socialist elements in Czechoslovakia, *Pravda* said on September 26, would have enabled NATO troops to "come up to the Soviet border, while the community of European socialist states would have been split."

On November 13, in an address to the Fifth Congress of the Polish Communist Party, Brezhnev expressed the Doctrine in its broadest and most authoritative form:

> When internal and external forces hostile to Socialism attempt to turn the development of any Socialist country in the direction of the restoration of the capitalist system, when a threat arises to the cause of Socialism in that country, a threat to the security of the Socialist Commonwealth as a whole—it already becomes not only a problem for the people of that country but also a general problem, the concern of all Socialist countries.

The lesson for the West was a sobering one. As long as we were visibly afraid of the competition of coexistence, the Soviets found advantage in talking it up. But to them it always seems to have meant a frozen *status quo* in Europe, including two Germanies and a clear sphere of Soviet influence in Eastern Europe. For some years their fundamental assumption has been that any change in things as they are would be to their disadvantage, and their analysis was probably correct.

Only when the Western Europeans and their transatlantic NATO partners began to talk in earnest about bridge-building, and act in earnest too, did it seem to dawn on the leaders of Russian communism that détente was bound to be deeply disruptive to the *status quo* in Europe. Since the Soviets prefer what is to what might be, they eventually had to decide that real détente was too dangerous. And in August in Prague, they made it plain with tanks and terror that the efforts of Dubček's regime to build a "socialist humanism" at home and freer relations abroad went well beyond the narrow limits of Soviet tolerance for change in Eastern Europe. Thus the most far-reaching lesson of the invasion of Czechoslovakia was that the Soviet leaders were newly afraid of détente, afraid of the contagion of competition with the West, and still, after 50 years of communism, afraid of the virus of freedom.

*   *   *

The politics of Western hope was rooted in the conviction that the Soviets really thought their interest ran with peaceful coexistence. The rationale for bridge-building, cultural exchange, and reciprocal political visits was the underlying assumption that the limits of tolerance in Moscow would permit the highly differentiated impulses in Eastern Europe toward independence, toward internal reform, toward easier and closer relations with the West to bring about gradually, erratically, but certainly a sea change in the climate of East-West relations. This process was seen as a prerequisite for negotiating an East-West agreement to reduce the large armed forces facing each other in Central Europe, and for a renewed effort to tackle the fundamental issues, centering on Germany and Berlin, which have divided Europe for more than two decades.

The action of the "Warsaw Five" in Czechoslovakia was a deep but by no means fatal wound to the agreed Western policy of pursuing détente by tiny steps. During the last ten days of August every NATO country hastened to dampen contacts, postpone political visits, and generally defer the building of bridges from West to East. The Minnesota Band did not visit the U.S.S.R., the Red Army Choir was not heard in England, and the Mayor of Moscow was shipped hurriedly out of The Hague. Ministers in half a dozen Western countries who had been preparing trips designed to bolster their personal contributions to peace, suddenly discovered urgent business at home. Diplomatic parties celebrating Polish Army Day, the Bolshevik Revolution and the like were boycotted by all but minor officials. The Italian fair in Moscow went on, but when in a show of business-as-usual the top Soviet leaders turned up as visitors, they found no Italian official of comparable rank had made the trip.

All these moves were the product of quick instinctive agreement, made explicit in political consultations at NATO head-quarters in Brussels. In the fall of 1968, nobody wanted to be accused of acting chummy with the Warsaw Five. At the same time the contacts with Rumania and Czechoslovakia, as well as with Yugoslavia, were stepped up; by early 1969, the increased contacts with those three countries more than offset, in NATO's running count, the sharp drop in contacts with the invading Five.

After a few months the shock effect of the invasion wore off, and it no longer seemed that the Czech affair was one of a series that might include Rumania and Yugoslavia. Nevertheless NATO's political leaders and their analytical staffs began to reassess their policy of pressing the Soviets and their communist allies for negotiations about mutual force reduction and a more permanent peace regime for Central Europe. Apart from beefing up the NATO defense system, the easiest conclusion was that prospects for a system of European security by agreement with the Soviets had been postponed into the unforeseeable future. The long run had clearly been lengthened.

One early political effect was to erase as wholly academic the long-standing question about the future of the Alliance after 1969. Even before the invasion of Czechoslovakia, it was apparent that no NATO ally was seriously proposing to avail itself of the provision by which signatories of the North Atlantic Treaty could, after the twentieth birthday of its coming into force (that is, after August 24, 1969), give one year's notice of withdrawal from its obligations and protections. (Some commentators seemed to believe that the Treaty by its terms needed to be renegotiated or reconfirmed by governments after twenty years, but that was never required, nor was it ever suggested by any government. As with the United Nations Charter, the members probably could not today get agreement on so clear and comprehensive a document if they were to start again from scratch.) Some allies, notably the Canadians, were thinking hard about how to carry less than their share of the common defense, a goal which France (by withdrawal) and several others (by holding down defense spending) had already succeeded in accomplishing. But by 1968, the betting around NATO was that even France, after its own special fashion, would stay in the Alliance.

The Czech crisis moved up the moment at which the "after 1969, what?" question could be safely raised. At the Brussels meeting in November 1968, the same one that collected pledges for more European defense effort, all fifteen Foreign Ministers provided the authoritative answer. Secretary Rusk arrived at the meeting fresh from a White House meeting with President-elect Nixon, who had been chosen in the election only a few days before. The Secretary promptly let it be known that it was firm bipartisan policy for the United States to stick with NATO "for the foreseeable future," and that we would be prepared to say so formally if others would. Skirting the kind of formal commitment that would constitute an amendment to the Treaty, and would therefore have required a vote of confidence in fifteen legislatures, the Ministers declared on November 16, 1968: "The North Atlantic Alliance will continue to stand as the indispensable guarantor of security and the essential foundation for the pursuit of European reconciliation. By its constitution the Alliance is of indefinite duration. Recent events have further demonstrated that its continued existence is more than ever necessary."

At a French-American breakfast that morning, French Foreign Minister Michel Debré had decided to adapt some 1966 language of General de Gaulle to add that "unless events in the years to come were to bring about a radical change in East-West relations, the French Government considers that the Alliance must continue as long as it appears necessary." That masterpiece of ambiguity could have been played as a dissenting footnote, but Debré agreed to have it stand as part of the communiqué itself, which made it possible to interpret it as French concurrence with the three sentences agreed by the Fourteen. The U.S. delegation therefore spread the word to the press that the French sentence was what would, in our Supreme Court, be called a "concurring opinion"—that is, agreement with the majority conclusion but for differing reasons. The American wire services reported our version of what had happened, and we waited with fingers crossed to see whether the French delegation would deny our interpretation in their own press backgrounding. But they let it pass, and the French sentence went into history as concurrence with the judgment that the continued existence of the Alliance was more than ever necessary.

*   *   *

If the Alliance was in business for an indefinite and probably lengthy future, what would be the content of its program? It was easy for Ministers in November 1968 to disagree with Brezhnev's Doctrine, and they did so with a good deal more verbal vigor than is par for ministerial communiqués in international organizations: "The contention of the Soviet leadership that there exists a right of intervention in the affairs of other states deemed to be within a so-called 'Socialist Commonwealth' runs counter to the basic principles of the United Nations Charter, is dangerous to European security and has invitably aroused grave anxieties."

It was also easy to agree that, as General Eisenhower used to say, "there is no alternative to peace." But in November 1968 the August shock was still too recent and the military implications too absorbing, to enable governments to think analytically about the implications for détente. They could agree only to re-endorse nonintervention and the U.N. Charter, point again to the defense-cum-détente doctrine of the Harmel *Report*, register the setback to earlier hopes, confirm that "in view of the action of the five members of the Warsaw Pact, the scope and level of Allied contacts with them have had to be reduced," declare without specifics that "consistent with Western values the political goal remains that of secure, peaceful and mutually beneficial relations between East and West," and recognize in general terms the need for détente management: "the pursuit of détente must not be allowed to split the Alliance."

But how were these principles to be extruded as policy? When and how and where should bilateral contacts with the Warsaw Five be turned on again? How long should the period of mourning for Czechoslovakia be? What would happen to the Federal

Republic's *Ostpolitik*, and all the bits and pieces of détente, from technology to friendship, that were in negotiation before the invasion? In the changed military circumstances, did the Reykjavik offer to negotiate about balanced and mutual force reductions still stand? When, and with what changes in mood and method, would the Americans reschedule their talks with the Russians on strategic arms control?

These questions could not be faced in a hurry. Stage Two of the Western reaction to the invasion of Czechoslovakia would await the Twentieth Anniversary Ministerial meeting of the North Atlantic Council in April 1969 in Washington, where the Treaty was signed April 1949.

Meanwhile the Soviets, having zigged with military force in Prague, zagged back to détente politics in Budapest. In March 1969, from a Warsaw Pact meeting in the Hungarian capital, the Soviet Union and its allies revived their proposal for a meeting of European states to fashion the future of Europe. The Budapest appeal was better dressed than at its earlier debut, wrapped in the chilliest of cold war accusations against the West, at a Bucharest meeting in 1966. Omitting most of the polemical finery this time, the Warsaw Pact statement claimed that "personal meetings" had shown that "not a single European government is opposed to the idea of an all-Europe conference" to discuss security and peaceful coexistence. This may well have been true in a way; the normal Western parry to the Soviet suggestion of a big peace conference had been to say that would be just fine—some other time after all sorts of preconditions had been met. The communists had some preconditions of their own; the Budapest appeal mentioned "the immunity of existing frontiers within Europe, including the Oder-Neisse frontier, and the borders between East Germany and West Germany, recognition of the existence of East Germany and West Germany, and that West Germany give up the demand to represent the entire German people, or for any form of possession of nuclear weapons."

A close reading of the Budapest appeal suggested a hard-fought compromise: the Soviets got their appeal, which they needed to divert public attention from their invasion of Czech-

oslovakia; the East German and Polish "hawks" got the preconditions on which they had been insisting; and the Czech
and Hungarian "doves" managed to delete most of the traditional
polemics. But after the Budapest meeting, each of the Warsaw
Pact governments buttonholed its special friends in the West,
to emphasize that the appeal was serious, not to be dismissed
as propaganda. The Russians even spread the magnanimous word
that they would not insist on the exclusion of the United States
and Canada if all the Europeans wanted them invited. That
was an important hint. NATO governments had agreed in the
North Atlantic Council that a conference on European security
with the U.S.S.R. present and the United States absent was
unacceptable, and except for Gaullist France, they had not been
reticent about saying so out loud.

Often in politics, questions of substance come disguised as
questions of procedure; certainly in diplomacy the heart of the
matter is nearly always what to do next. Approaching their
Washington meeting, the Foreign Ministers of the NATO nations
did not have to decide whether they really wanted to hold
a European Security Conference, let alone consider what positions to take in preparing for it. Their problem was a narrower
one: what to say about the Budapest appeal at the NATO meeting April 11, and how to explain what they did there to their
own publics on April 12. Some of them were sorely tempted to
come out strongly for a European Security Conference, in order
to sound as "forthcoming" as possible in the ears of their own
peace-minded electorates. Old Socialist Pietro Nenni, who was
serving briefly as Foreign Minister in a precarious Italian coalition, was one of these.

The case for such a move is not to be lightly dismissed; as
we have seen, a similar tactic had been one key to getting
practical disarmament talks under way in the early 1960s. A
word about the nature of the Soviet ploy may help clarify the
political dilemma debated by the NATO Ministers in Washington.

It is quite easy, and almost riskless, to *look* as though you
are trying hard to make peace if you stick to procedural proposals: suggesting publicly where two litigants might meet, or
offering yourself to meet with your adversary. Not long after

the Budapest appeal, the Finnish government got into the act by suggesting Helsinki as a meeting place; this move, described by its authors as the most important foreign-policy initiative taken by Finland since World War II, did not require any thought about what such a meeting might accomplish, and did not even commit Finland to the judgment that holding it would be a good idea. Other recent examples of this valuable technique were Kosygin's willingness to host an India-Pakistan peace meeting at Tashkent; U Thant's 1964 suggestion that the U.S. meet secretly with representatives of Hanoi at the Burmese capital of Rangoon; General de Gaulle's insistence that peace in the Middle East could come only if the Big Four, including France, discussed it together; the Reykjavik offer by NATO to discuss mutual and balanced force reductions in Europe (an offer made before any concentrated work had been done by the allies on the substance of the problem); and the traditional stance of each American President that he will travel anywhere if peace will be served thereby.

I am not suggesting such postures and proposals are useless. Sometimes, as in the Tashkent case, they are very useful indeed. But a proposal for a meeting can be very misleading if it is taken as the moral equivalent of a peace proposal—our long siege at the Paris peace talks on Vietnam bears witness. As soon as some important people are scheduled to meet somewhere about something, a great public expectation develops that something important must be happening or is bound to happen. That is not always, or indeed often, the case. High-level meetings bathed in publicity are best reserved for situations in which the participants already know what is going to happen, and attend not to negotiate an agreement but to unveil and celebrate it.

In the spring of 1969 the subject of European security was nowhere near ripe for a big conference. The Soviet Union and its partners therefore were risklessly proposing a conference of European states at which a grand settlement of Europe's deep and divisive trouble would be negotiated. Nearly every one knows that this is not the way things work in the real world. Complex and long-standing security issues which touch the vital interests of every NATO ally, every member of the Warsaw Pact, and every European neutral as well—issues such as the division of Germany, the Berlin anomaly, the mutual and balanced reduction of forces in Europe, the free movement of people and goods, and, above all, the free play of ideas—such issues would be sharpened, not settled, by the circus atmosphere of a big international conference, unless they had been worked out ahead of time, step by step, behind the scenes, by all the nations (including of course the United States) which would need to participate in the final settlement.

For that very reason the kind of conclave the Russians were pushing was unlikely to happen soon, if ever. A more practical technique of multilateral negotiation would be a number of conferences on manageable chunks of the European security problem, among those nations which have some reason to be there, with provision for enough advance preparation to make sure the outcome was an agreement, not a big disappointment. But it was of course the very impracticality of the Soviet scheme that made it a safe proposal for the Soviets to make—and which, so some Western Ministers argued, made it safe for NATO to advocate too.

If the Soviets themselves had not intervened clumsily in the process, the Ministers celebrating NATO's twentieth birthday would probably have found it politically wise (in view of the domestic pressures on them) to mention the Budapest appeal in their final communiqué. They might have balked at welcoming it, but they might well have noted it as an interesting idea worth exploring with the Soviet bloc countries on how to get on with practical steps toward a permanent peace. Even the U.S. delegation was in a position to go that far. After convening the National Security Council to debate the dilemma, the President had sent to the Secretary of State a short directive for the delegation's guidance. It was a model of clarity in policy-making, which contained both a summary analysis of the issue involved and a formula for its resolution: we could accept the principle of an eventual conference but should stress the need for talks on concrete issues, and for NATO consultations to develop coherent Western positions on them.

But then the Russians suddenly took a series of hardline actions that changed the atmosphere, persuading even those who were most anxious to give Soviet sincerity the benefit of the doubt that to adopt a position parallel to the Budapest appeal would look gullible in the East and silly in the West.

As a prelude to the NATO meeting in Washington, which had been publicly scheduled for months, the Soviet Navy conducted in the Atlantic Ocean the largest naval exercise they had ever put on there, using 21 warships and 8 submarines. Just to be sure that even the Mediterranean members of the Atlantic Alliance got the point, nearly all of these ships after the maneuvers passed through the Straits of Gibraltar to bring the Soviet Mediterranean squadron up to the greatest strength (more than 50 warships) the growing Russian presence had yet achieved in that narrow sea.

Then, for those who had been too busy to connect this military demonstration with the debate at the Washington meeting on how to make peace with the Russians, the Kremlin leadership issued on the day before the NATO session a long, strongly-worded polemic—not just a propaganda article in *Pravda* or *Izvestiia* but a formal statement issued through the news agency TASS by the government of the Soviet Union—berating the Alliance, all its members, and all its works in language reminiscent of the early 1950s.

The Soviet statement fell like a great stone into the Ministerial meeting. The abusive text first became available as a dispatch in French from Agence France Presse. While we were still summarizing it in English at our corner of the conference table, I watched the AFP ticker item hit the other delegations, passed from Minister to Minister with whispers of shock and disbelief. I could almost feel the temperature drop in the big air-conditioned State Department conference room. Why, I asked myself, do the Soviets so often slap the West across the face with a dead fish just when peace-seeking publics have brought governments to the point of doing something that might bring negotiations nearer and push war farther away?

Perhaps the timing was casual: the Kremlin obviously had to issue some statement to try and take the edge off NATO's birthday party; the writers of standard polemics had been routinely told to draft something, the document had been circulating for clearance in the Soviet bureaucracy, and just happened to collect its last initial on that crucial day. That would be the charitable interpretation, charitably attributing to the Kremlin a capacity for interfering with the achievement of its own purposes which is observable from time to time in our own big government. But another interpretation is more probable—that the Soviet leaders, fearing that NATO was about to come out for a European Security Conference and make some practical proposals on how to get there, began to see how disturbing to the *status quo* in Europe such an enterprise might really be. And so they punctured the balloon of Western hope, which they know from experience just how to do.

Even the most sentimental NATO Ministers, and those with the most yearning constituencies, were struck dumb by the dead fish from TASS. They did not want to reopen the cold war by answering the Soviet statement in kind; but in the circumstances they could hardly welcome the Budapest appeal either. So they omitted in their communiqué to mention either one, and concentrated instead on how to engage the Soviets and their Warsaw Pact allies in negotiating some "concrete issues." After all, one of them remarked at the White House dinner that night, just as honesty is the best policy in business, so in international politics a real willingness to move toward peaceful settlements should be the best propaganda for peace.

*   *   *

The participants in the Washington NATO meeting were well prepared to think concretely about "next steps" in East-West relations. Throughout the winter and early spring of 1969, the Foreign Offices of the Alliance and the representatives in Brussels had been trying to figure out what the tanks in Prague had done to their pre-invasion policy of "peace by osmosis," as Secretary General Brosio liked to call it. If each step toward loosening internal controls in East Europe or improving relations with the West was likely to produce another turn of the repressive screw in the East, what could the NATO allies do about it in good conscience and with some prospect of success?

The answers were provided not by foreign-policy analysis but by the shifting currents of domestic politics. In most NATO countries, during the winter of 1968–69, we began to observe a confluence of hard-liners and soft-liners on a common policy: let's get on with détente anyway, even if we thereby make the Soviet leadership uncomfortable. Those politicians more inclined to wish-thinking wanted to get back to their proven vote-getting formula, the politics of peace gestures. But they were now joined by many who had scoffed at détente as a mushy-headed policy threatening the maintenance of an adequate defense: since the Czech crisis had shown that the Soviets were alarmed about détente, there must be somthing in it after all. In between these extremes, the people who had always thought defense and détente had to be part of a single policy saw a massive consensus forming around the "two pillars" of the Harmel *Report*.

During February and March 1969 the full-time NATO consulters in Brussels fashioned this consensus into words: 6,000 words in French and English, agreed by fifteen governments in the only way diplomats know how to agree, by appointing instructed representatives to slog through a text, paragraph by paragraph, day after day, week after week, drafting and redrafting, translating and retranslating, an alchemic process, one part genius and nine parts tedium, that has only one redeeming quality—it works.

The alchemists were members of the Senior Political Committee, a group of North Atlantic Council deputies which worked intensively for several weeks, longer than it takes to draft most treaties, producing the document which after detailed analysis in fifteen capitals and further arguments among the fifteen Ambassadors to NATO, was presented for adoption to the Washington meeting. The quality of this document—its relevant recommendations, its closely reasoned supporting analysis, and its comparatively lucid style—is remarkable for a paper which had to be internationally agreed. To have reached the same result through normal diplomatic channels without the "zero" of multilateralism would have taken . . . the thought is too appalling to pursue. In any event, it is probably fair to say that it represents a high-water mark in the practice of consultation. For those familiar with the document in question who may not think its standard of relevance and literacy all that high, I hasten to make clear that it is not a patch on what a single informed individual could have written in one-fiftieth the time, working all by himself in the dead of night. But the NATO paper has this advantage: it is a statement of common policy by fifteen governments.

The conclusion of this process of political wordsmithery was that there is simply no alternative to trying to make peace with the Soviets in Europe. Pursuing this aim, while keeping our powder dry, is the only way to do something practical about peace and freedom in Europe. But the prospect for getting back on the road toward improvement in the East-West climate—and beyond that, toward agreed and dependable security arrangements in Europe as a whole—was deeply shadowed by the very fact of the Soviet invasion of Czechoslovakia, no matter what happens next in that country. The demonstrable Soviet allergy to man's natural instinct for freedom would for some little time force NATO to concentrate, more than its members would prefer, on the peacekeeping side of its dual personality, while its latent peacemaking function would await better days and brighter prospects. The allies still wanted "practical arms control," but even "during an era of negotiation the defense posture of the Alliance should not be relaxed. . . . The maintenance of effective defense is a stabilizing factor and a necessary condition for effective détente policies."

The Permanent Representatives on the Council then proposed several pages of "Policy Guidelines," with the suggestion that Ministers meeting in Washington agree that all their governments would follow them. In reopening East-West contacts, the allies would continue to differentiate between the Warsaw Pact invaders and the others; they would do their best to talk peace, but they would also continue to reject any Soviet right to domination of Eastern Europe or to intervention in the Federal Republic under the United Nations Charter.

On East-West negotiations, the allies welcomed President Nixon's intention to restart arms talks with the Russians, since the President intended to consult in the Council on the subject. In approaching an "era of negotiation," attitudes were important: any East-West talks should be carefully prepared, should relate the several issues to each other, and should avoid illusory reactions to the zigs and zags of Soviet coexistence policy. On the Budapest appeal, a Conference on European Security could only be held when there was some prospect of settlements, especially on the German question; meanwhile it was best to stick to practical next steps. The Alliance would, however, continue the study of longer-range issues of a European peace, in line with the Harmel *Report*.

The guidelines on Alliance consultation echoed the Nixon commitment, especially its "before and during" feature. When it comes to European peacemaking, the allies would try to agree not only what, but also whether and how, to negotiate. They would of course go deeply into strategic arms issues and other matters which touch East-West relations in Europe.

The Fourteen then appended a reminder that their powder should be kept dry in an era of negotiation; reaffirmed the Reykjavik appeal for talks about mutual force reductions in Europe, and described once again the kinds of forces that were needed to convert these principles into trained men and modern hardware in a rising market.

Agreement on these "Policy Guidelines" was probably the most important thing that did happen at NATO's twentieth anniversary meeting. The action took only a few minutes, but that is not to be wondered at. Precisely because it was so important, the decision could not be left to the whim of political Ministers, many of them representing only one party or tendency within a coalition Cabinet. In multilateral diplomacy, when Ministerial actions are important they are cooked in advance.

There was a last minute flurry of dissent from the French delegation; this too is traditional. In recent years, a good many Foreign Ministers have left town just before the communiqué is drafted because they find the arguments with the French, on major points of policy disguised as minor points of translation, so enervating. The standard French tactic is to claim, with the natural authority accruing to the representative of Molière and Victor Hugo, that a policy statement with which France disagrees cannot be rendered in the French language. It is a weapon of devastating potency in a communiqué-drafting committee. NATO has repeatedly been saved from linguistic paralysis only by the fact that André de Staercke, the Belgian dean of NATO's Ambassadors, himself uses the French language with such elegance and loving care that his suggestions cannot be spurned as "Anglo-Saxon."

On this occasion the French Minister suggested that the Council merely "note" the "Policy Guidelines," treating them as an interesting exercise by subordinates but not as agreed governmental policy. Secretary of State Rogers, steering between "adopting" and "noting" the Guidelines, suggested that each government take them into account in its own actions, which (at least in English) seemed the moral equivalent of adoption. On that understanding the Guidelines were approved.

Once the Guidelines were pasted on the Western bulletin board, it remained for the Ministers to celebrate the twentieth anniversary by turning on another "study"—which meant another political negotiation among them, to be conducted once again through the representatives at NATO headquarters in Brussels:

> Ministers recalled that one of the essential aims of the Alliance is the establishment of a just and lasting peace in Europe, based on stability, security and mutual confidence. The Allies propose, while remaining in close consultation, to explore with the Soviet Union and the other countries of Eastern Europe which concrete issues best lend themselves to fruitful negotiation and an early resolution. Consequently, they instructed the Council to draft a list of these issues and to study how a useful process of negotiation could best be initiated, in due course, and to draw up a report for the next meeting of Ministers. It is clear that any negotiations must be well prepared in advance, and that all Governments whose participation would be necessary to achieve a political settlement in Europe should take part.

As this is written, the list is being debated in Brussels and a proposal to loosen things up between East and West Berlin is in the works. Progress is unlikely to be sudden. But the sense of direction set by consultation is reasonably clear: the Western allies will (in further consultation with each other) promote détente, without expecting that their promotion will be taken by the communists as a comradely act.

The Russians may have the raw power to contain for a time the growing desire of many, probably most, East Europeans for the decencies of freedom and the niceties of life. But repression cannot indefinitely smother expectations which are produced not by NATO's machinations but by the yearnings of people for a more humane society—nourished, to be sure, by the lively example of more liberal life in the West. A cartoon in a Paris newspaper, during the autumn of 1968, managed to say it all in a single caption. It showed a group of students and workers standing on a street corner, discussing politics with animation. In the background, two Russian commissars are wringing their hands, and one of them is saying to the other: "The trouble with all these people's democratic republics is that they seem to be producing democratic republican people."

Chapter IX

The Allies Beyond NATO

It seems unlikely that in the 1970s the future of NATO and an East-West settlement in Europe will be the most pressing items on the world's headache agenda. On the contrary, the attention of Americans as citizens of a world power is more liable to be riveted on their discontents and divisions at home; on relations with Asia, and the strength and role of China, in the aftermath of the Vietnam war; on food, population, and an increasingly intolerable gap between rich and poor; on the overseas impact of our own progress in race relations; on how to build prosperity in a world of shaky moneys; and on how to keep the peace in a world of nuclear spread.

Our European allies share some of these concerns. They have their own malaise and military at home. They have their own specialized worries about turbulence in portions of the globe to which they are tied by history or sentiment. They are active in monetary management and aid for developing countries. They are all signatories of the Charter and members of the United Nations. And while comparatively inactive in Asia they are not unconcerned with war and peacekeeping there. Before suggesting how the North Atlantic allies might tackle the future of Europe, therefore, it may be useful to ask how serious are their consultations outside the "NATO area."

*　　　*　　　*

In 1956 NATO's Committee on Non-Military Cooperation (the "Three Wise Men") declared that the Alliance "should also be concerned with harmonizing their policies in relation to other areas, taking into account the broader interests of the whole international community." In spelling out the reasons for advocating this course, the Wise Men wisely did not predict that NATO would fold up if it did not perform this supplementary task; the reasons they adduced for global concern sounded more like surface public relations than underlying necessity:

> In following this course, NATO can show that it is more than a defense organization. . . . It can prove its desire to cooperate fully with other members of the international community in bringing to reality the principles of the Charter of the United Nations. It can show that it is not merely concerned with preventing the cold war from deteriorating into a shooting one; or with defending itself if such a tragedy should take place; but that it is even more concerned with seizing the political and moral initiative to enable all countries to develop in freedom, and to bring a secure peace for all nations.

Similar sentiments have been repeated in every NATO self-study, including the Harmel *Report*.

In practice, Alliance consultation has not in fact been limited by geography. The North Atlantic Council discusses any subject on earth, or indeed in outer space; its meetings and subcommittees range over the Middle East, Africa, Asia, Latin America and the planets. Discussions about the NATO defense system or about the political future of Europe are designed to lead to consensus on action to be taken, often action by the organization itself; whereas, on other topics, the discussions are usually labeled "exchange of information." At most, they are designed to lead to parallel national actions, not international action.

Within these limits this Western political caucus can sometimes perform a useful service by stressing a common political solidarity in fields where the rivalries and tensions among allies are more apparent. Consultation in the North Atlantic Council helped make sense of the debate about a "technological gap" between Europe and America; it could be helpful in working out transatlantic monetary and financial arguments; it may be useful in helping the allies to deal with their social problems at home. And Alliance consultation can certainly continue to be useful, if not decisive, in "harmonizing" national attitudes and aligning national policies beyond the perimeter of NATO defenses.

*   *   *

During the 1960s there was a rash of criticism of the expanding scope of American business in Europe. France in particular had trouble getting used to the idea that, for example, the French subsidiary of International Business Machines was the country's third largest industry. Jean-Jacques Servan-Schreiber's *Le défi américain* (The American Challenge) quickly became a best-seller in 1967 not so much because it pointed to the embarrassing comparative inefficiencies of European industry as because of its brilliantly demagogic title. The gap in understanding and analysis of the problem was even greater than the gap in management methods and computerized systems. Some Europeans were advocating a Marshall Plan for Technology, as though technical progress could be crated, shipped, and unloaded ready-made. Some Americans were embarrassed and defensive, wondering whether they were welcome in Europe at all.

At Italian initiative, the technology gap was brought into the North Atlantic Council as a topic of political consultation. It proved to be a highly successful example of what organized transatlantic conversation can accomplish—bridging, if not the differences in technical know-how, at least the gulf of nonsense and misunderstanding that had come to dominate the debate. After serious study all the allied governments were willing to agree, in the Council, that the gap called "technological" is more a problem of basic education, management training, entrepreneurship and enterprise than it is an absence of channels for the transfer of technology as such. After that, and some serious and detailed work in the Organization for Economic Cooperation and Development and in the European Economic Commission, more and more Europeans could be heard to say that, since the Americans can hardly be expected to slow down their own rate of growth while Europe catches up, the main thing for Europeans to do about the "gap" is to speed up their own growth through harder work, broader educational opportunities, more enterprising enterprise, closer integration, riskier investments, and, especially, undertaking more of their own research and development. The good sense heard on both sides of the Atlantic on this subject was partly produced by a deliberate process of professional consultation in the political Council of the Alliance.

To deal with economic and financial issues, the North Atlantic allies usually meet together in wider organizations in order not to exclude from equal status the various kinds of European "neutrals" (Sweden, Switzerland, Austria, Spain) and the industrialized nations of the non-Atlantic world, notably Japan and Australia. The organizations are plural: the Organization for Economic Cooperation and Development (OECD), successor to the OEEC of Marshall Plan fame; OECD's Development Assistance Committee (DAC), which tries to make coordinated sense of the $7 billion in development aid which flows from the rich countries to the poor countries each year; the General Agreement on Tariffs and Trade (GATT), venue in the 1960s for the Kennedy Round of tariff negotiations; and the Group of Ten moneyed nations whose Finance Ministers and central bankers have been meeting increasingly often to stabilize the world's money markets, negotiate about each other's exchange rates, and support the price of gold.

It is evident that when these international organizations are at their best, they operate by continuous negotiation. Periodic flurries of consultation at moments of crisis do not engage the long-term political interests of the members. Too often, in these wider and briefer meetings of specialists, there is lacking the sense of a common political purpose, which in matters of security has held the North Atlantic allies together through their tests of cohesion.

The success of NATO's Nuclear Planning Group in converting "nuclear sharing" from a transatlantic expletive to an allied experience argues for analogous treatment in economic and financial matters. The cases are different, of course: somewhat different groups of countries are involved, and the United States does not have the dominant position in trade or money that it has in nuclear weaponry. Nevertheless in commercial relations, for example, we would do well to develop a system for intimate and continuous, not arm's length and sporadic, negotiation about how much discrimination the transatlantic trade rivals will practice against each other. Real participation by the Europeans in the management of the dollar as an international currency might save us literally billions of dollars in what we now think of as balance-of-payments trouble.

In the Kennedy Round of tariff reductions, the Common Market countries bargained collectively with the United States for mutual trade concessions; but this was a one-time bargain. On our side, it had to be authorized by a special Act of Congress, the passage of which was President Kennedy's most hotly debated achievement in the 1962 session of Congress.

On the European side, the negotiation was equally traumatic. The modest mutual concessions finally worked out after five years were only agreed among the European participants after the deadline for agreement had passed in the summer of 1967. By then, both sides to that unimpressive bargain, the European Common Market and the United States government, were so intellectually exhausted and politically bankrupt that neither has since thought seriously about another such effort. Yet prosperity on both sides of the Atlantic requires continuous efforts to chip away at tariff walls and at those nontariff fences—quantity quotas and internal taxes—which are not effectively subject to bargaining among the industrialized countries at all.

In monetary policy, the deficit in the U.S. balance of payments is serious mostly because the other main industrial countries (essentially, NATO allies and European neutrals, plus Japan) are not yet willing to hold enough additional dollars each year to offset our deficit. They could probably be persuaded to do so if they were cut in on the management of the dollar, on the not unreasonable assumption that the dollar is now their main international medium of exchange as well as ours. But that is still heresy in Washington. It would involve foreigners being explicitly consulted about decisions we have always regarded as "domestic"—the setting of interest rates, the regulation of demand, the management of the federal budget and the public debt. Here again, the dilemma of consultation is how much American discretion we are willing to trade for how much European performance.

We have not yet decided to make our own national discretion an explicit bargaining counter in an international negotiation (even though our internal tax and money policies are in practice heavily influenced by what foreign treasuries and central bankers say and do). We are therefore paying heavily in gold and goodwill for the absence of a satisfactory transatlantic monetary bargain.

*　　　*　　　*

As the North Atlantic Alliance started its third decade, its leaders were acutely aware they confronted not only adversaries abroad but adversity at home. In every society voices were raised to question whether what is established is worth defending. The East-West confrontation which brought NATO into being suddenly was seen to have a new dimension.

Those Western earth tremors of the late 1960s—*les évènements de Mai* 1968 in Paris, the closing of the universities in Italy, the riots in West Berlin, and, in America, the unique combination of student and racial violence—found seismic echo in Warsaw and Prague, and even (in more muted form) in Kiev and Moscow. In Eastern Europe, as in the West, a generational gap of crisis proportions opened up, in which the young rejected the rhetoric of the cold war and yearned for something better than life by bureaucratic regulation and ideological slogan. If the West had its New Left, the East had its New Right, both equally against their home-grown Establishments.

The stand-off between the more-or-less democratic West and the more-or-less communist East in Europe was thus expressed not only in missiles, machine tools, and meat products. Social policy and the struggle to build humane institutions amidst spectacular new technologies had come to be part of the confrontation too.

In his first trip to Europe as President, Richard Nixon met with groups of selected citizens in each major country; the discussions in these groups, unlike the official talks with Prime Ministers and Foreign Ministers, turned to worries about the social fabric, the human costs of technological change, the sometimes violent dissatisfactions of youth. To the surprise of his foreign-policy advisers, the President thereafter insisted that the North Atlantic Council start a serious consultation on "environmental" issues. At first the Foreign Offices of the allied countries resisted the idea as beyond NATO's pale; but as their political bosses thought hard about the idea, they agreed to try a consultation on the umbilical connection between domestic turbulence and international disorder.

When he spoke to the NATO Ministers at the twentieth anni-versary session of the North Atlantic Council in Washington on April 10, 1969, President Nixon made it official:

> . . . I strongly urge that we create a committee on the challenges of modern society . . . to explore ways in which the experience and resources of the Western nations could most effectively be marshalled toward improving the quality of life of our peoples.
>
> That new goal is provided for in Article 2 of our Treaty, but it has never been the center of our concerns. Let me put my proposal in the context of our times:
>
> On my recent trip to Europe, . . . our talks turned to those matters deeply relevant to our societies: the legitimate unrest of young people, the frustration of the gap between generations, the need for a new sense of idealism and purpose in coping with an automating world.
>
> These were not subjects apart from the concerns of NATO; indeed, they went to the very heart of the real world we live in. We are not allies because we are bound by treaty; we bind ourselves by treaty because we are allied in meeting common concerns. . . .
>
> The Western nations share common ideals, and a common heritage. We are all advanced societies, sharing the benefits and the gathering torments of a rapidly advancing industrial technology. The industrial nations share no challenge more urgent than that of bringing 20th century man and his environment to terms with one another—of making the world fit for man, and helping man learn how to remain in harmony with his rapidly changing world.
>
> We in the United States have much to learn from the experiences of our Atlantic allies in their handling of internal matters: the care of infant children in West Germany; the "new towns" policy of Great Britain; the development of depressed areas programs in Italy; the great skill of the Dutch in dealing with high-density areas; the effec-tiveness of urban planning by local governments in Norway; and the experience of the French in metropolitan planning.

Having forged a working partnership, we all have a unique opportunity to pool our skills, our intellects and our inventiveness in finding new ways to use technology to enhance our environments, rather
than destroy them. . . . This could become the most positive dimension
of the Alliance, opening creative new channels to all the rest of the
world.

The Nixon initiative was not, strictly speaking, an exception
to the tradition that NATO will stay out of its members' internal
affairs. It was intended to provoke an altogether new kind of discussion, a new dimension of "consultation." The idea is to learn
from each other (using the North Atlantic Council as a convenient forum for the educational process) what works best in dealing
with the enigma all industrialized societies seem to be facing:
What is it about our institutions that produces so much dirt,
congestion, ugliness, unfairness, turbulence, crime and terror?
Unlike the other topics of NATO consultation, these "environmental" issues are not put up for bargaining, even among close
friends and allies. Any resulting action is to be domestic; only
the conversation is to be international. But the conversation
should reflect a shared opinion that if these questions do not
get a satisfactory answer in the Western democracies, the "internal" issue whether democracies are worth defending will
suddenly become a more proximate threat than the armed forces
of any external enemy.

The President's proposal was picked up, by prearrangement,
in the communiqué issued by the NATO Ministers from their
twentieth anniversary session.

> The members of the Alliance are conscious that they share common
> environmental problems which, unless squarely faced, could imperil
> the welfare and progress of their societies. The Ministers recognize
> that important work on these problems is already being carried out
> within other international organizations. The Ministers instructed
> the Council in Permanent Session to examine how to improve, in
> every practical way, the exchange of views and experience among the
> Allied countries, whether by action in the appropriate international
> organizations or otherwise, in the task of creating a better environ-
> ment for their societies.

This nugget of bureaucratic prose started NATO officially on
a most unbureaucratic innovation. By the autumn of 1969 a

Committee on the Challenges of Modern Society was in business, a "ginger group" (as one British diplomat called it) with Daniel P. Moynihan of the White House staff providing the ginger from the Washington end. Once the political reluctance to talk about each other's "internal affairs" was overcome, the problem was to choose among the dozens of topics crying for attention in every allied nation. The interests of the allies, Moynihan declared after meeting with them,

> deal with the degradation of the environment through pollution, the complex interaction of technology on individual and group; the compelling issues of nutrition; the pressing matter of population growth and the use of space. . . . the impact on modern society of the automobile, . . . the whole matter of inadvertent weather changes and . . . ocean pollution, for the North Atlantic itself is no more immune to environmental degradation than the now pathetic streams that once proudly flowed by the great cities of our nations.

It would be rash to predict what will become of all this, but it would be no more than prudent to suggest that unless the North Atlantic allies are able to come to grips with relevant subjects like these, the peacekeeping and peacemaking tasks of their Alliance will lose much of their hold on the populations of the member nations.

*   *   *

When it comes to peace-and-security issues geographically beyond the "NATO area," most of the North Atlantic allies have their own pet preoccupations. Portugal has its African territories; Greece and Turkey their Cyprus impasse; the United Kingdom its Gibraltar and its East of Suez trauma; Belgium its Congo, the Netherlands its Caribbean troubles; France its overseas Francophones, and the United States its ties to Latin America, Asia and other areas. Discussion of these topics in the North Atlantic Council is essentially one-sided consent-building, which is among the paler forms of "consultation." By keeping our allies informed and providing timely explanations of what we are trying to do in Vietnam, for example, we purchase a degree of surcease from government-sponsored criticism of U.S. policies, and pass along the ammunition our allies need to tranquilize the more vociferously anti-American elements in their own politics.

This is a stricter interpretation of the allies' common interest than NATO's founding fathers and Wise Men had in mind. Throughout the 1950s and into the early 1960s, there was still a hope that the Common Market might lead to a Western European political union that could in time develop a post-colonial European foreign policy in partnership with (while keeping its distance from) NATO's North American partners. As the 1970s began, the ambitions of the "good Europeans" were much more limited. They were hoping to recover from the long Gaullist block to integration by dealing their British and Nordic neighbors into a broader but shallower unity; most of them accepted the reality that building a wider club would postpone indefinitely the achievement of a supranational Europe with a common defense, a unified foreign policy, and an integrated nuclear force of its own. Earlier in the 1960s there had also been hope that the Soviet leaders might be lured to calm their fears of the West and loosen their grip on Eastern Europe. Czechoslovakia and the Brezhnev Doctrine had postponed that prospect too.

Meanwhile, the pattern of world politics left little room for the inward-looking Europeans. As the Vietnam conflict wore on and wore out, a major shift in Western relations with Asia became not only possible but necessary, but from Europe it seemed likely that Asians, who had outlasted the Americans in war, would also shape the resulting peace. Most Europeans felt equally powerless to affect the outcome or assuage the bitterness of the chronic conflict in the Middle East. U.S.-U.S.S.R. relations featured direct discussions on Vietnam and negotiations on the Middle East, and on arms control issues ranging from a seabed nuclear ban to a freeze on nuclear missiles. Thoughtful Europeans, even those with the broadest world view, had come to feel helpless and irrelevant: "The world is afire," said Raymond Aron in a bitter commentary about the Arab-Israeli war, "and we are preoccupied with beets."

Failing the unification of Europe, the individual nations could pretend to be world powers only by attaching themselves as tails to the American kite—or by the kind of political prestidigitation that no European leader save de Gaulle had the talent to attempt. In the United States many former advocates of a European world role came reluctantly to the conclusion expressed in 1969 by McGeorge Bundy, former assistant to Presidents Kennedy and Johnson:

> Nothing in my own failures of perception over the last twenty years is more striking, as I look back, than my inability to foresee the degree to which the role of Western Europe would be reduced in other continents. . . . it is far from clear that Europe has been wrong in her renunciation of power abroad. All I am saying is that something very important has happened here—that it has happened progressively and rapidly through the last decades—and that in the main it seems irreversible. . . .
>
> The war ended the notion of distant power for Germany and for Italy. The peace has ended it for France and Britain. . . . Europe can now have no decisive foreign policy except that of the future of Europe.

*   *   *

There are three main exceptions to the general rule of embarrassed silence in the North Atlantic Council on peace-and-security issues arising outside the NATO defense perimeter. One is any change in the bilateral relations between the United States and the U.S.S.R. Another is anything that touches the Mediterranean; yet another is the "grey area" of European countries not members of NATO yet potentially threatened by a Soviet policy of force.

The Council is at its most lively and loquacious when bilateral relations between the two superpowers are up for consultation. Our allies know that when it comes to creating a more permanent European security system and settling the "German question," the key question is what the Americans and the Russians can agree on. To most NATO governments and their Permanent Representatives in Brussels, the most interesting questions about any issue arising outside Europe—Vietnam, Mideast, Kashmir, Cuba, or whatever—are the Soviet role and the U.S. role in dealing with the Soviets. The prevailing attitude is ambivalent: our NATO allies want U.S.-U.S.S.R. "détente" and a settlement of critical issues, yet fear the prospect of two superpowers reaching decisions that have the effect of a *diktat.* All other American-Soviet relationships they regard as tests for the ultimate negotiation about Europe. In every NATO consultation about U.S.-Soviet talks on whatever subject, this is the "hidden agenda."

The most important current test case of consultation on U.S.-U.S.S.R. relations is the much-deferred negotiation on the limitation of strategic nuclear missile systems. Here we are thoroughly committed to consult with our allies on the substance of our position. It is a reasonable promise for us to have made, since we will be talking about limiting the strategic deterrent on which (in the interest both of nuclear non-proliferation and of increased conventional defense effort) we have assured the Europeans they can absolutely count.

The chronic state of war or near-war in the Middle East naturally engages the continuous attention of the allies not only because war so nearby is obviously dangerous but also because the regional rivalries provide such opportunities for Soviet penetration. The Arab-Israel conflict produced the only overt military action against the forces of a NATO ally in the first twenty years of the Treaty—the inadvertent air attack on the *Liberty,* an American intelligence ship operating in the Eastern Mediterranean and therefore inside the NATO defense line. It occurred to no one to invoke Article 5 of the Treaty; but the incident illustrated how clear and present is the danger to NATO from warfare so close at hand.

Despite the dangers, the NATO allies admit to differing interests, and most of them are reluctant to be committed to common action in the Middle East. Popular sympathy for the Israeli cause is widespread in Europe; but Turkey, Italy, France, and Germany, which (for widely varying reasons) have been cultivating the Arabs, prefer a posture of strict neutrality and tend to regard U.S. policy as dangerously pro-Israeli. After the Soviet invasion of Czechoslovakia and the sharp NATO reaction to it, Israel took the occasion to suggest direct consultations between itself and NATO on "Mediterranean security"; the suggestion was politely turned aside. A NATO consultation about the Middle East typically ends with an exhortation to support the efforts of the big powers and of the United Nations to achieve a durable peace settlement.

Two strategic islands in the Mediterranean, Cyprus and Malta, were part of the NATO defense area while they were still British colonies, but as independent states and U.N. members they are now, in a sense, non-NATO enclaves. Three times in the decade of the 1960s Greece and Turkey almost went to war over Cyprus; they were restrained in part by their common interest as members of the Alliance. During the last and most dangerous of these near-wars, President Johnson sent Cyrus Vance as a conciliator. Vance's efforts were reinforced by Secretary General Brosio, who worked quietly and effectively in Athens and Ankara with a mediation mandate from the North Atlantic Council, stressing the dangers to the Alliance and helping the Turks and Greeks to back away without backing down.

Malta has a "special relationship" with NATO: it is host to a NATO military command, and by Council resolution and exchange of letters, NATO and Malta are to consult whenever the island's security is threatened. The open-ended Malta Group consults about aid and investment to Malta from NATO countries, and also provides a convenient place for considering the dangers of Soviet fleet visits and political penetration.

The least-discussed non-NATO Mediterranean country is Spain. For thirty years Spain has been ostracized from European politics; most of the Western governments actively helped the Spanish Loyalists in 1937, and much of Europe's political leadership is still deeply resentful of Franco's durable victory. Spain's military geography became even more important when General de Gaulle threatened to exclude the Alliance from French territory, and the United States gently pressed the notion of associating Spain somehow with the NATO defense system. The answer came back loud and clear: talk to us when Generalissimo Franco is no longer around. Another obstacle to Spanish membership is the ugly issue with Britain over the Rock of Gibraltar, one of the United Kingdom's few remaining colonies; but that issue might conceivably be settled by relating the Rock to a NATO of which both Britain and Spain were members. These political deterrents to Spanish membership in NATO have been controlling; in the 1970s, political change inside Spain might well enable the other Europeans to bring it into the security club. From the standpoint of an effective security system in the Mediterranean, that would clearly be the rational thing to do.

The invasion of Czechoslovakia brought into sharp focus the dilemma of the Alliance which has drawn a sharp defense line, yet obviously wants to avert adverse changes in the balance of power beyond that line. Studying the effect of the Soviet intervention in Prague, analysts felt that NATO should do something to warn the Soviets against a continuing policy of force in East and Central Europe. Each potential case was different from all the others. Threatened Rumania was after all a Warsaw Pact member, unlikely to draw much Western support to its physical defense. The Yugoslavs would probably fight for every inch of their mountains, as they did against the Nazis in World War II; and some Western governments would be inclined to help them against the Russians as they did against the Germans. Austria is the subject of a State Treaty, the violation of which would require some military reaction by the Western signatories, including several NATO members. Finland, operating in the shadow of Soviet power, prefers not to be the object of NATO contingency planning.

In the end, the NATO Ministers at their November 1968 meeting found a way of warning the Soviets without specifying what actions the Soviets were not to take, which countries they were not to take those actions against, or what NATO would do about it. It is the nature of political deterrence that the vaguer the warning, the more effective it is likely to be. In a tone of voice normally reserved for declarations about Berlin, fifteen Foreign Ministers were thus able to agree to the famous "unclear signal" of November 16, 1968:

> The members of the Alliance urge the Soviet Union, in the interests of world peace, to refrain from using force and interfering in the affairs of other states.

> Determined to safeguard the freedom and independence of their
> countries, they could not remain indifferent to any development
> which endangers their security.
> Clearly any Soviet intervention directly or indirectly affecting the
> situation in Europe or in the Mediterranean would create an inter-
> national crisis with grave consequences.

These words did not mean, as some newspapers said at the
time, a formal extension of the NATO defense line to include
European neutrals. It was no more, nor less, than an accurate
prediction of Western reaction if the Soviets turned from talk
of coexistence to a policy of force in Europe. Once again, NATO
members were saying that while they might not always work
together elsewhere, Europe is home and will be treated accordingly.

*   *   *

Beyond the Middle East and the "grey area" of Europe, the
reluctance of allies to consult on joint or parallel action varies
directly with the distance from themselves. By this calculation,
the Far East is still very far away. When I arrived in Europe during the autumn of 1965, the major escalation of American involvement in Vietnam had just begun; most European governments thought it a mistaken path even then, and were not bashful about saying so. By 1967, our allies had stopped giving us
advice about limiting our efforts in Vietnam. They were convinced by our military efforts that the United States was sufficiently determined not to be thrown out of South Vietnam by
force, and they were persuaded by U.S. peace proposals and peace
missions that President Johnson really wanted to get out of South
Vietnam by negotiation. Not wanting to tell the United States
to abandon what the Americans regarded as a commitment to be
fulfilled, our European allies sat back to watch us extricate ourselves from what they still regarded as our unilateral war. Thereafter, my colleagues in the Council contributed not with their
advice but with their silence, treating our Council briefings as a
source of facts and ideas to use in facing down those who used
the U.S. predicament in Vietnam as an anti-government ploy in
their own domestic politics.

After Vietnam, what? Depending on the nature of the ultimate settlement in Southeast Asia, some of our NATO allies might be willing to help with peacekeeping forces or development aid; both will be sorely needed. But if we want to multilateralize the next stage in Vietnam, if we will want "more flags" in the postwar arrangements, if we want to share the obligations and costs of peace and development, we will need to consult early and often with those whom we would hope to involve. NATO itself cannot be an actor on a Southeast Asian stage; but what we have learned about the Golden Rule in NATO consultation should come in handy as we try to fashion a reasonable peace in the Far East.

After-Vietnam consultations might lead to deeper study of Europe's interest in China's future policies. Already China is a mystery and a menace of growing concern to thoughtful European leaders. The hopes that China's strength will make Russia more cooperative with the West (on the reasoning that "the enemy of my enemy is my friend") are beginning to be offset by concern about Chinese capacity to threaten North America and Europe with intercontinental missiles. The United States will be worrying about China in any event, during the generation to come. It will be in the American interest to include our transatlantic partners in the community of the concerned.

Chapter X

Alliance with a Future

There was a time when the dawn of peace was equated by some with the death of alliances. The doctrine was that "blocs" are bad for peace; the way to achieve peace in Europe was therefore to work toward eliminating "both blocs." Even the Soviets were suggesting that the Warsaw Pact could be abolished if the Western allies would only agree to jettison NATO.

This doctrine never garnered much real support, except from Eastern European leaders who saw it as a way to loosen their ties with the Soviet Union. Gaullist France played with the notion verbally, while avoiding actions that would have made the words come true. Outside France, opposition parties ritually echoed the anti-bloc line, but in NATO's first twenty years the argument was not successfully pressed as a major election plank in any Western nation.

One trouble with the doctrine of mutual pactocide was that NATO and the Warsaw Pact are not at all parallel, in content or constitution. The Eastern alliance is a means of control, the Western Alliance is a method of consultation.

NATO has an international military defense system. The Warsaw Pact has had no integrated staffs, even for planning; its operating headquarters is simply part of the Soviet General Staff. NATO has peacemaking functions—a doctrine of détente, a way of discussing arms control negotiations, a civilian Secretary General with predominantly a civilian staff. The Warsaw Pact's political function is limited to occasional meetings of Communist Party or governmental leaders. The Pact's "Secretary General" is an official in the Russian Foreign Ministry who also has other things to do. NATO is a free association of sovereign nations, the Pact is a mandatory bloc. Some of NATO's members do not like the way others manage their internal affairs, but the North Atlantic defense system is not a Holy Alliance, available to invade them on that account. Using the Warsaw Pact, the Soviets have declared a special relationship with other countries in that web they call a "socialist commonwealth," the special relationship of the spider with the fly. As in the spider's web, it is easy for nations to enter the socialist commonwealth, but forbidden to depart.

In a nutshell, the Warsaw Pact's adversary is an international alliance called NATO, but NATO's adversary is really the Soviet Union.

If both alliances were abolished, what difference would it make? An enormous difference—a change in the balance of power profoundly to the advantage of the Soviet Union. The Russians would remain in charge of East European armies, and could keep their troops in Eastern Europe under existing bilateral agreements. But without NATO or something very much like it, the basis for a U.S., British, and Canadian presence on the Continent would be destroyed, along with the basis for the arrangements with Germany that make German military strength acceptable to its Western neighbors. Each European country, in isolation from its friends, would have to make its bilateral security arrangements with the U.S.S.R., and its political antenna and internal political alignments would shift accordingly.

The growing clarity on this subject in the West has greatly reduced the number of European politicians and journalists who would model Alliance policy on what happens in the Warsaw Pact. They have come to see that even if the Warsaw Pact were to abolish itself—which is even more unlikely now that the Soviets have rediscovered its value as an ally-suppressing device—we would still need a Western solidarity organization. We would need it for defense. We would need it to induce the Soviets to bargain realistically about European security and the German question. We would need it to help keep honest whatever East-West bargains can be struck in Europe; mutual trust is best rooted in the capacity of each side to make sure the other is keeping his agreed word. For as far ahead as the eye can see, therefore, a Western solidarity organization will be part of the East-West landscape in Europe. Whether, in time, people call it NATO will be a matter of taste. Whether they call it necesary could be a matter of destiny.

*   *   *

Three main questions will be permanently on the agenda of this Alliance-with-a-Future, whatever its label. The transatlantic allies will be bargaining about how to maintain a credible defense while credibly seeking to make peace with the Russians in Europe; what to settle for in a "European settlement"; and how to negotiate it with the Soviets and their Eastern European allies.

In answering each of these questions the policy of the United States is, for better or worse, the key. A credible defense depends on the U.S. presence in Europe, which in turn engages the nuclear deterrent. In a European settlement the Soviets and Americans, as the two major outside factors in "the German question," must come to terms. Washington is (from the Soviet standpoint if not from NATO's) Moscow's "opposite number" in peace negotiations.

The recent record, detailed in earlier chapters, suggests it is not beyond belief that the North Atlantic allies can maintain a modern defense and still try for détente. It will take fortitude, which the West has in abundance, and patience, of which the West is chronically in short supply. The resolve to stay with the strategy of deterrence until the Soviets are ready to negotiate about Europe may be eroded by ennui in Europe or enervation elsewhere, as in Vietnam. But if we posit that the West will have the courage and good sense to stay the course and make a negotiated outcome possible, then what is meant by "European settlement" and resolution of the "German question"? And how do we reconcile East-West entente with Atlantic cooperation?

The traditional models, by which we have lived and talked these twenty years past, are certainly too vague and too contradictory for uncritical carryover into the 1970s. Indeed the story related in this book—how history's closest peacetime allies stuck together despite détente, disillusion, and de Gaulle, by practicing the art of consultation—seems curiously detached from the debate about ideal structures which has been going on in universities, planning councils, and journals during the 1960s. That debate has featured three competing ideas: the unity of Western Europe, the union of the Atlantic allies, the reunification of Germany. But the Atlantic idea was always overmatched against its European rivals. Despite all the advocacy of unity in Western Europe—some of the most enthusiastic voices spoke with an American accent—the Common Market has been stalled, and the European defense idea is at best a footnote, not a major theme, of this period of history. While the proponents of Atlantic union succeeded in collecting general endorsements for an Atlantic constitutional convention, they were more persuasive in lobbying for NATO than for more far-reaching but less probable institutions.

German unification is also more mentioned in despatches from pundits across the Atlantic than advocated by practitioners of diplomacy in Central Europe. In four years and hundreds of official contacts with fifteen NATO governments, I did not meet a single uncompromising advocate of German unity. On similar pretexts but for shared reasons of fear and distrust, Germany's Western European neighbors—the French, the British, the Italians, the smaller allies—have lost whatever enthusiasm they may once have had for the project. Even those German leaders who profess to foresee a single German nation have been notably willing to postpone that objective indefinitely in favor of Alliance solidarity and East-West détente.

If the great themes of the Grand Design have been curiously irrelevant in the 1960s, will they prove equally inapplicable to the 1970s? They probably will—and for the same reason. As long as Soviet intransigeance obscured the contradiction, the reunification of Germany could be safely advocated in the same breath as Western European integration and Atlantic solidarity.

But as soon as we think seriously about a European system negotiated with the Soviets, the contradictions emerge all too clearly: if Germany is unified, Western Europe will not be integrated and the Atlantic Alliance will no longer be solid.

It therefore seems likely that the new Grand Design will have as its centerpiece the kind of Germany that the Western allies can advocate without undercutting their other declaratory policies. Such a Europe of the 1970s would be a ragged but potentially stable system:

- Two Germanies, politically distinct but linked by internal trade and freer travel.
- A settlement of outstanding frontiers to reduce as much as possible irredentist claims that threaten the general peace.
- An arrangement for Berlin that guarantees access to and from a Free City. (Twenty-five years of postwar history cannot be unrolled, and Berlin cannot become part of a recognized East Germany.)
- Permanent peacekeeping arrangements, to include both international inspection and a sufficient U.S./NATO presence to keep the deal honest. (Between great powers the only dependable peacekeeping device is a closely supervised balance of power.)
- A regional arms control agreement, featuring:

—Balanced and phased reductions or redeployments on both sides, involving both local and outside forces in Central Europe. (Merely reducing U.S. and Soviet forces, and leaving West Germans glaring at the East Germans, might produce *more* instability than at present.)

—Reduction or elimination of the Soviet ballistic missiles targeted on Western Europe. (This will be possible only in the context of the wider Strategic Arms Limitation Talks between the United States and the Soviet Union, and might affect the deployment of some theater nuclear weapons in a trade-off.)

—Agreements renouncing the use of force in Europe, confirmed perhaps in a formal multilateral nonaggression pact.

—Measures to reduce the threat of surprise attack or accidental war. (These might include military liaison missions on both sides of the line between NATO and the Warsaw Pact, with mobile observation posts, freedom of movement and reporting, overlapping radar screens, and even direct communications links between local military headquarters in West and East Europe.)

In effect, this "settlement" would trade our rhetoric about the unification of Germany for a European security system that would be more dependable and less expensive, plus a more solid arrangement for access to Berlin. This kind of détente is not ideal from anybody's viewpoint. It leaves Europe semi-divided and partially armed. But the apparent alternative of a "real" détente in Europe presupposes a Soviet Union no longer interested in dominating its East European neighbors, which is a cold war outcome as improbable as it is devoutly to be wished. And the true alternative—the *status quo* without agreement and without disarmament—is even less attractive.

*   *   *

Who on the Western side negotiates for the allies? Once things get serious, each nation will want to be present when its interests are affected. That means some two dozen countries are potential parties to every major negotiation. Are there ways of conducting a practical negotiation among two dozen nations at a time?

There are, because this negotiation need not be one but several. Indeed, it is quite impossible to imagine an East-West bargain about Europe being struck all at once. It would probably be the consequence of a whole series of conferences about European security, rather than a grand European Security Conference, as put forward by the Warsaw Pact members. In such a context different techniques may be useful for different purposes at different stages of the game.

In the early stages of probing to ascertain if the Soviets are serious, it does not matter very much who conducts the inquiry; small countries are indeed well-placed to do so, as Belgian Foreign Minister Harmel was among the earliest to perceive, since the Soviets would not mistake (for example) a Belgian suggestion for a NATO proposal.

To make sure the interests of all the Western allies are protected in establishing procedures for negotiating, the Secretary General of NATO might well be empowered to deal with the Warsaw Pact nations for the purpose, checking back through the North Atlantic Council with the allied governments as necessary. In practice, this would be a negotiation with the government of the Soviet Union, which would doubtless wish to serve as spokesman for all the Warsaw Pact members. But it would be best for NATO not to seem to "recognize" the Soviets' control over their European allies; consequently, the Secretary General would have to touch base with all the Warsaw Pact capitals, as well as those of the European neutrals who would want to be consulted about procedures for working toward a better European security system. There would be the traditional objection, especially from Paris, against "bloc-to-bloc" negotiation. But the realistic alternative to the NATO Secretary General is the United States, acting as surrogate for its allies. Would Paris prefer that?

Some subjects, notably the control of strategic nuclear arms, lend themselves to direct bilateral talks between the United States and the Soviet Union. Yet the issues to be negotiated bilaterally are close cousins of the issues in a European settlement. That is why it is so important that the U.S. government consult frankly, early, and often with its NATO allies whenever their future security is engaged.

Any arrangements about the future of Germany must of course be formally agreed among the Four Powers (United States, the U.S.S.R., Britain, and France) with "special responsibilities" growing out of World War II. A wider circle of nations is nevertheless very directly affected by the German question, and any such settlement would have to cut them in on the making of decisions; both their national security and their defense forces will, after all, be deeply affected. Eventually all NATO and Warsaw Pact members would have to be involved, together with all the various shades of European neutrals, each of which (Finland, Sweden, Switzerland, Austria, Yugoslavia, and Spain) has unique interests of its own.

A panel of private American citizens assembled by the United Nations Association proposed early in 1969 that the Four Powers should establish a European Security Commission composed of ten countries; on the Western side, Britain, France, Italy, the Federal Republic of Germany and the United States would be members; on the Eastern side, a degree of recognition would be accorded to East Germany by seating it as a full member along with Poland, Czechoslovakia, Hungary, and the Soviet Union. The Commission would "prepare the general principles of a European settlement"; then the Four Powers would authorize West and East Germany to negotiate between themselves a whole scheme for settlement, including acceptance of the Oder-Neisse line as Germany's eastern frontier, the provisional acceptance of the division of Germany, and "the eventual reunification of Germany." Meanwhile, the wider Commission would be trying to negotiate "the military posture and arms control safeguards of the NATO and Warsaw Pact and focus in a region wider than but including Czechoslovakia, Poland and the two parts of Germany."

An alternate procedure would be for the North Atlantic Council as a whole to propose the establishment of a standing Conference on European Security which could include all members of NATO and the Warsaw Pact, and such of the European neutrals as wished to join. (Calling it the Conference on European Security rather than the European Security Conference would help make clear that NATO's transatlantic partners were both necessary and welcome.) The Conference itself would meet seldom, and only to ratify arrangements already worked out in smaller groups or through diplomatic channels. But it could serve as an umbrella for special-purpose conferences among smaller groups of nations on manageable chunks of the European security problem.

*   *   *

A generation of peace in Europe has been accomplished not by sketching a grand design but by following a grandly civilized procedure called Alliance consultation—perhaps the farthest advance in practical cooperation among still-sovereign nations. The priceless ingredient of any acceptable East-West transaction is that the Western allies hang together in negotiating it.

Looking ahead to the 1970s, a wide range of subjects will have to be sorted out with our allies, multilaterally and bilaterally, informally then formally, early rather than late. They include the transatlantic bargains on financing, providing, and managing forces for deterrence and defense; nuclear planning issues; arms control and disarmament policy, including strategic arms limitation; the management of East-West relations in Europe; the search for a better European security system; an eventual resolution of the "German question"; trouble in the Mediterranean, the Middle East, and beyond.

On all these subjects the North Atlantic Council has become a standing diplomatic conference which offers its members a chance to influence each other's attitudes and actions—to penetrate each other's policy-making machinery—and to do something practical about the loneliness that comes with their international responsibilities.

There is no general rule that enables the United States or any of its fourteen Atlantic allies to maximize its opportunities in the consultation process, or totally to avoid complaints about not consulting promptly, fully, and frankly. But there is one simple question which—if asked automatically, early enough, and at a high enough level—illuminates the case for consultation and helps keep the option of cooperative action from being prematurely or thoughtlessly closed. The litmus test is this: *How would we react if one of our allies behaved as we intend to behave, without consulting us about it?*

The Golden Rule can be found in the ethics of half a dozen world religions. It is not surprising to find it useful in a secular alliance as well.

Notes

Some of the opinions and concepts in these pages have seen the light of day in magazine articles while I was working for the U.S. government in Europe. I am particularly grateful to *Foreign Affairs, The Saturday Review, Interplay,* and *The Atlantic* for the relevant permissions. I have not, however, resisted the temptation to rewrite these ephemeral writings in the light of later events or maturer judgments.

*   *   *

There are so many references in this book to the doings of the North Atlantic Council that a word may be in order about its ground rules, or their absence. Unlike the political bodies of the United Nations (the Security Council and the General Assembly), the North Atlantic Council has no written rules of procedure, never takes a vote, and seldom passes a Resolution; in my 45 months on the Council, I saw fewer than a dozen formal Resolutions. The North Atlantic Council operates "by consensus," which means the Council's Chairman draws from the discussion a summary which, if no Representative objects, becomes the Council's decision. The process is therefore something like a jury or a Quaker meeting: until there is general agreement there is nothing.

This arrangement does give a strong-willed nation or even a strong-minded Representative a considerable advantage—up to a point. But it does not seem to operate in such a way that the term "veto" applies. If one nation objects too much, or for too long, the others usually find some way to go ahead together anyway. In the case of the French withdrawal, the Fourteen did so by constituting the Defense Planning Committee as the Council for defense purposes; this was done with the acquiescence of the French Representative, but in such a way that he did not have to give positive assent (which would have required the explicit approval of General de Gaulle, and that was then in doubt).

The law on this subject is fuzzy, and is kept that way by common consent. No sovereign nation wants to concede in peacetime that it belongs to a club which can act in its name without its permission. But in practice the consensus procedure requires only silent acquiescence, a willingness to let an opportunity for objection go by; it does not require an affirmative vote. Since the U.N. Security Council can act even when a Permanent Member abstains (or is absent), it is not to be supposed that the North Atlantic Council has less authority to act in the interest of the collectivity under comparable conditions.

Suppose that most of the allies decided it was important to use a nuclear weapon but that one country not directly threatened and not involved in NATO's nuclear planning (Iceland, Luxembourg, Portugal) were reluctant. That certainly would not restrain the others from acting, or even from announcing that their action was in support of NATO obligations. Indeed, the obligation in such a case would be to recognize that an attack on NATO is an attack on all; but the Treaty leaves quite open what each nation will do about it. The consensus action in such a case would be a statement by the Chairman that all members except X, Y, and Z proposed to act in a certain way, that no unanimity had been achieved, but that those directly threatened and those possessing the means to act had better do what they think they have to do, and have so indicated in the Council.

In many cases of individual holdouts from a Council consensus, the minority of one has a special problem in its domestic politics, and wishes by its dissent not to prevent the collectivity from acting but to pacify its own public opinion. In these circumstances that country's Representative in the Council is often quite happy to make his objection loud and clear, and let it be known to his own press that he has done so.

Even in a case of NATO action short of reacting under Article 5 of the Treaty to an armed attack, the same principle of flexibility would in practice apply. For example, Norway, Denmark and Canada would be unlikely to participate or even positively to agree if, in a situation short of war, the allies with forces in the Mediterranean wanted to activate the On Call Naval Force. But they would be equally unlikely to try to tell their allies that they should be as uninterested in the security of the Mediterranean as Canada and the Nordic nations traditionally are. Ditto, the other way around: Turkey might not come to the rescue should a situation short of war occur in northern Norway or the Danish island of Bornholm (a favorite spot for theoretical war games), but the Turks would hardly try to tell Britain or the United States to be equally relaxed.

In its naked form the veto question has never been sharply posed or tested. Nor has there been a practical test of a more recherché question: If a Council member walks out of the chamber in a huff, can those who remain continue to act as the Council? The French agreed to the DPC arrangement to avoid facing that question in the negotiations with the Fourteen. The only other case in my experience occurred when the Greek representative threatened to walk out of the Council if the Danish representative persisted in an effort to bring before the Council the issue of democracy, or rather its absence, in Greece. Since the Danish representative was able to get his instructions softened in time, the

Greek threat was not tested, and the Chairman did not have to rule on whether the remaining fourteen members were the North Atlantic Council or an informal rump session of some kind. Again, based on U.N. Security Council practice (which is far from a good analogy but is the best we have), my own judgment would be that the North Atlantic Council can and should survive the political absence of one of its members.

*   *   *

I have avoided cluttering this informal narrative with footnotes that might create the illusion of scholarship. This book is not a research monograph; it is a policy monologue. Speeches and government reports that are readily available in standard sources of reference are not further identified. It may nevertheless be useful to identify some documentary sources and provide some fuller explanation here and there.

Chapter II   *The Golden Rule of Consultation*

The quotations from the North Atlantic Treaty and other basic NATO reports can be found in the NATO *Handbook*, which is reviewed and republished from time to time at NATO Headquarters, Autoroute Zaventem, Brussels 18, Belgium. The 1951 citation was quoted in the 1956 Report of the Three Wise Men.

The first set of "Wise Men," in 1951, was mostly concerned with burden-sharing among the Atlantic allies; the principals in this negotiation were Edwin (now Sir Edwin) Plowden of the United Kingdom, Jean Monnet of France, and W. Averell Harriman of the United States. The second application of this negotiating formula, in the mid-1950s, found Lester Pearson of Canada, Halvard Lange of Norway, and Gaetano Martino of Italy studying the Alliance's nonmilitary functions. Their Report, adopted by NATO governments in 1956, contains the most comprehensive legislation on Alliance consultation.

The quotation about unilateralism and the war in Vietnam is from James K. Thompson's contribution to a symposium on "No More Vietnams," held at the Adlai E. Stevenson Institute in Chicago and reprinted in *The Atlantic*, November 1968 issue. A fuller version of the point I make here about our need to act multilaterally in order to justify overseas commitments in our domestic politics can be found in "The Road Back to Internationalism," *The Atlantic*, May 1969. A more comprehensive case for multilateral action is contained in my chapter, "The Future of International Politics," in Walter J. Ong, ed., *Knowledge and the Future of Man* (New York: Holt, Rinehart and Winston, 1968).

The development of techniques for full-time consultation through the North Atlantic Council owes much to the four men who held the post of NATO Secretary General (and Chairman of the Council) during its first twenty years. It is a measure of the importance the allied nations have attached to this Alliance that all four of them—Lord Ismay of Britain, Paul-Henri Spaak of Belgium, Dirk Stikker of The Netherlands, and Manlio Brosio of Italy—have been outstanding people, who had served at high levels in their own governments before their selection by NATO. It will not be easy for the Alliance in its third decade to maintain this high standard of leadership.

Chapter III   *The Doctrine of Deterrence*

The "big bombs" remark by President Kennedy is cited by Theodore Sorensen in *Kennedy* (New York: Harper & Row, 1965), p. 625.

Chapter IV   *The Sharing of Nuclear Uncertainty*

On the birth of MLF: George Ball, who was Undersecretary of State at the time, says the project for a multilateral nuclear force was "conceived as an educational instrument and a healing ointment to relieve the pressures for proliferation; it was also—and this was perhaps the crucial consideration in most of our minds—a means of strengthening Western cohesion in a testing time for our common civilization and political purpose." George W. Ball, *The Discipline of Power* (Boston: Little, Brown & Co., 1968).

On the death of MLF: McGeorge Bundy, who wrote the recommendation to President Johnson that ended U.S. support for the project, explained his own change of heart in a frank and revealing lecture at The Ditchley Foundation in England on July 18, 1969:

> I had my share in the effort to construct and market the MLF, and all I can say in my defense is that in the end I also had my share in shelving it. It was an effort to square the nuclear circle, and it could not work. What has worked best, in the end, has been what is simplest: first, the fact of American men and weapons on the spot, and second, the growing fact of serious discussions of nuclear policy—both of them based on the reality of ultimate responsibility.

Bundy's conclusion on the nature of influence in nuclear issues is from his Ditchley lecture, as is the later remark on strategic superiority.

The early history of the Nuclear Planning Group, and the analysis of the issues it considered, is essentially based on what was told to the press by U.S., British, German, and other spokesmen in open press conferences or "background sessions" at the time. The rules of the "backgrounding" game are not wholly clear. In effect, anything said by a government official to a group of newspapermen, which they are told they can use on their own authority without attribution to the government or the official, must be considered as having been declassified.

Thus, for example, the public total of U.S. nuclear warheads in Europe was 7,000 for some time. But after Secretary of Defense Clark Clifford twice used the figure 7,200 in discussing them with the press on a background basis, the latter figure began to be publicly accepted. It did not mean the United States had added 200 weapons to its nuclear stockpile.

However, it would be clearly beyond the rules of the game to quote with attribution from the transcript of a press backgrounder, without the explicit permission of the official involved. I am grateful to former Secretary Robert McNamara for such permission in connection with this chapter.

It is usually hard to pinpoint a moment of Presidential decision, but President Kennedy made up his mind about General and Complete Disarmament on his motor launch off Hyannisport, just before the lunchtime Bloody Marys, on August 5, 1961. Arthur Schlesinger's version in *A Thousand Days: John F. Kennedy in the White House* (Boston: Houghton Mifflin Co., 1965), pp. 478–79, corresponds with my own recollection of how it came about.

The Khrushchev letter on missiles in Cuba has never been published in its entirety. The quoted passage, however, was reproduced by Elie Abel in *The Missile Crisis* (Philadelphia: J. B. Lippincott Co., 1966), p. 161, Mr. Abel sought and received the acquiescence of the State Department for this use of it.

The figures on strategic nuclear forces come from congressional testimony by Secretaries of Defense Robert S. McNamara and Clark M. Clifford. They are assembled and analyzed in George W. Rathjens, *The Future of the Strategic Arms Race; Options for the 1970s*, a lucid pamphlet produced for the Carnegie Endowment for International Peace (New York, 1969).

The U.S. urge toward strategic missile talks during 1968 was right in line with American public opinion, even after the invasion of Czechoslovakia. A Louis Harris poll taken during October and November found Americans favoring U.S.-Soviet agreement to limit nuclear weapons systems by the decisive margin of 66 to 23 per cent. By 57 to 33 per cent, the Harris cross-section (5553 interviews) also supported a final summit meeting with Premier Kosygin before President Johnson left office. But about the results of these endeavors the same interviewees were not equally sanguine: by 48 to 40 per cent, they thought it "not possible" for the United States and Russia "to come to a long-term agreement to control wars in the world which will work." *Washington Post*, December 9, 1968, p. A21.

President Nixon's use of the word "sufficiency" reflected the prevailing view held by most students of strategy for some years past; the concept can be found in Secretary McNamara's speeches while he was in office and the writings of Dr. Henry Kissinger, who became President Nixon's Special Assistant for National Security Affairs. On January 27, 1969, a week after his inauguration, the President tempered a journalistic storm on the subject with these extemporaneous words at a press conference:

> Let me put it this way: When we talk about parity, I think we should recognize that wars occur usually when each side believes it has a chance to win. Therefore, parity does not necessarily assure that a war may not occur.
>
> By the same token, when we talk about superiority, that may have a detrimental effect on the other side in putting it in an inferior position and therefore giving great impetus to its own arms race. . . .
>
> I think "sufficiency" is a better term, actually, than either "superiority" or "parity."

Chapter V *The Western Defense Bargain*

The phrase "better measured by the clock than a calendar," and some of the figures and judgments in this chapter, are those of Timothy W. Stanley, who as Defense Adviser in the U.S. Mission to NATO educated me in the mysteries of strategic studies and systems analysis. But except where indicated in the text, he is absolved from responsibility for the way his pupil has used this education.

A useful comment on transatlantic cooperation in defense production and procurement is in Robert E. McGarrah, "Let's Internationalize Defense Marketing," *Harvard Business Digest*, April 1969.

Chapter VI *Tests of Cohesion*

The Kennedy quote is from Theodore Sorensen's book already cited; the President's reasoning is based on the account in Arthur M. Schlesinger, Jr., *A Thousand Days*, cited, p. 563. On the Kennedy-de Gaulle meeting, Sorensen's impressionistic picture (pp. 559–63) and Schlesinger's more systematic notes (pp. 349–58) are best read together for a rounded view of its setting and its substance.

In the matter of France versus the Fourteen, I have spared the reader most of the professionally fascinating political and legal complexities of the France-NATO relationship, including the interesting issue of financial claims. Those who wish to dig deeper in this rich mine of international law and practice should not miss the analysis by Professor Eric Stein of the University of Michigan and Dr. Dominique Carreau of the University of Paris, entitled "Law and Peaceful Change in a Subsystem: 'Withdrawal' of France from the North Atlantic Treaty Organization," *The American Journal of International Law*, July 1968. See also Carl H. Amme, Jr. *NATO Without France* (Stanford, Calif.: The Hoover Institution on War, Revolution and Peace, 1967).

Chapter VII *The Management of Détente*

Karl von Clausewitz' well-known definition of war, which I have adapted as a definition of détente, is from *Vom Kriege* (1833): "War is not merely a political act, but also a political instrument, a continuation of political relations, a carrying out of the same by other means." In a 1938 lecture Mao Tse-tung made a comparable remark: "War cannot be divorced from politics for a single moment."

Chapter VIII *The Politics of Peacemaking*

Early in the discussion of what came to be called the Brezhnev Doctrine, my German colleague on the Council, Ambassador Wilhelm Grewe, suggested a parallel with the doctrine of intervention propounded and enforced by the Holy Alliance or, rather, the political system Metternich organized at the Congress of Vienna. The analogy is strikingly apt.

Chapter IX *The Allies Beyond* NATO

The comments of the Three Wise Men are in paragraphs 32 and 33 of the Report of the Committee of Three on Non-Military Cooperation in NATO, 1956, reproduced in the NATO *Handbook*.

The figure of $7 billion, as the net flow of official resources from rich countries to poor countries, is close to the figures reported by the Development Assistance Committee of OECD for both 1967 ($7,034 million) and 1968 ($6,950 million). These represent net flow from DAC countries only, defined as gross disbursements minus amortization receipts on earlier lending. Private flows would add another $4,213 million in 1967 and $5,905 million in 1968. More detailed figures can be found in "Development Assistance: 1968 and Recent Trends," an OECD press release, Paris, July 11, 1969.

President Nixon's April 10 address, and the NATO Ministers' communiqué of April 11, 1969, are available in the public record. Daniel P. Moynihan's version of what the Committee on the Challenges of Modern Society might do is from his address to the North Atlantic Assembly in Brussels, October 21, 1969. An even more comprehensive earlier version is contained in an address by Robert Ellsworth, then

Ambassador-designate to NATO, at Westminster College, Fulton, Missouri, on May 10, 1969.

Chapter X *Alliance with a Future*

The proposal for a standing European Security Commission is contained in *Toward the Reconciliation of Europe: New Approaches for the U.S., the U.N., and NATO*, a Report of a National Policy Panel established by the United Nations Association of the United States of America, released on February 2, 1969. Chairman of the Panel was Theodore C. Sorensen; Henry A. Kissinger served as a member of the Panel until his selection by President Nixon as his Special Assistant for National Security Affairs.

Index